Paul Kalinauckas is Joint Managing Director of the Escatel Group, a performance-improvement consultancy which specialises in bringing coaching-based solutions to business issues. He was the subject expert for the BBC video *Coaching for Results* and has written several articles on coaching, as well as contributing to forthcoming books on *Managing Continuing Professional Development* and *Upside-Down Management*. He has worked as a professional coach in various organisations with individuals committed to improving personal and business performance. He has also run many coaching development programmes to build in-house coaching capability and is a visiting lecturer at the Universities of Oxford and Warwick. His expertise in coaching has led to him speaking at a number of international conferences in Hong Kong, Puerto Rico, Finland, Japan and Denmark. In regular demand as a consultant, personal coach and public speaker, he is widely recognised as being able to put his subject across in a highly participative and engaging manner.

Prior to being a coach he was the Secretary-General of the British Junior Chamber of Commerce; he then worked for a leading European training and development company on productivity improvement, customer service and quality. He now dedicates his time to building the coaching capability of the Escatel Group, training new coaches and writing on the subject. His personal vision is to be the leading exponent of coaching in the world, to continue to develop coaching processes and to act as a catalyst towards their implementation.

Helen King is a training manager in the leisure services industry and has over 10 years' experience of management and organisation development. At present with Pavilion Services, she has worked in several blue-chip companies such as Bass, Granada and the Automobile Association, where she introduced operational driven human resource initiatives. Besides developing and implementing a coaching and upward coaching process to assist organisations with cultural change, she has written management development and training programmes specific to team building, communication and behavioural aspects within organisations. She has also created a personal development planner based on a coaching, facilitation and leadership style that encourages people to be influential in their own development. Being at the sharp end of the business has enabled Helen to put her theories into practice, linking initiatives to operational and organisational requirements.

COACHING
Realising the potential

Paul Kalinauckas

Helen King

INSTITUTE OF PERSONNEL AND DEVELOPMENT

Typesetting by The Comp-Room, Aylesbury
Printed in Great Britain by
The Cromwell Press, Wiltshire

British Library Cataloguing-in-Publication Data
A catalogue record for this book is available from the British Library

ISBN 0-85292-555-7

**INSTITUTE OF PERSONNEL
AND DEVELOPMENT**

IPD House, Camp Road, London SW19 4UX
Tel: 0181 946 9100   Fax: 0181 947 2570
Registered office as above. Registered Charity No. 1038333
A company limited by guarantee. Registered in England No. 2931892

Contents

Acknowledgements

Charles Handy provided the initial inspiration and challenge to write this book. We would also like to acknowledge all those others who have contributed ideas and expertise. In particular we would like to thank John Ager, Jim Glover, Steve Goodman, Jeff Matthews, Brian Rees and Matthew Reisz for reading the drafts and making constructive comments for improvement, Barbara Howe, Ros Smith, Helen Starbuck and Nicola Turner for assisting with the production and our colleagues in Escatel Group and Pavilion Services Ltd. We would also like to thank Brooke Bond Foods Ltd, East Midlands Electricity, Gripple Ltd, Kalamazoo System Print, Motorola, National & Provincial Building Society, Office of Population Censuses & Surveys and Rover Group for enabling us to record some of their work in developing coaching capability. And finally a big thank you to all those extraordinary individuals with whom we have worked as coaches.

Preface

What was it about this book which first caught your eye? Our guess would be that it was the word 'coaching'. It is a word being used more and more in organisations. The purpose of this book is to provide a range of practical hints and tips to develop coaching skills. It has been written in response to the growing demand for more information on the subject and its applications in business. It is for managers who want to develop as coaches as well as personnel, training and human resources (HR) specialists. It has been designed for ease of use and outlines how to coach effectively. Although elements of the achievement coaching process may seem startling at first, do persevere. Sceptics may also like to examine the experiences of the well-known organisations described in the final chapter.

It is often the simplest things that have a major impact on an organisation, primarily because most people can understand them. Coaching, as you will discover in this book, is an inherently simple process. We are not suggesting that it is easy to put into practice or a simple panacea for all organisational ills. However it has produced outstanding results by talking with people, listening to them and gaining their commitment to accepting responsibility and taking action.

The book contains a menu of the coaching methods that have proved most successful in practice. You will be able to select those that best meet your needs. We hope that it provides you with new insights into coaching and encouragement to try them out.

Paul Kalinauckas and Helen King
August 1994

1
What Is Coaching?

Introduction

The purpose of this chapter is to clear up some of the confusion surrounding the word 'coaching', a word that is most commonly used in either a sporting or training context. Recent years have seen its arrival in the vocabulary of business and organisational development. We also hear coaching being associated with total quality management (TQM), competence development, staff empowerment, Investors in People and other such programmes.

Our general view of coaching is that it is 'a process to bring out the best in people'. However in our experience most people's understanding of the term seems to centre on some form of instruction. The coach instructs or demonstrates a particular skill or task to the 'trainee'. The trainee then has a go and receives feedback from the coach on their performance. The process appears to be:

1. Coach demonstrates the task.
2. Trainee practises carrying out the task.
3. Coach gives feedback and reviews progress.

However, as organisational structures have changed, so the role of managers has moved towards supporting rather than controlling. Traditional structures required a manager to control, command, direct and specify the work of subordinates. Modern organisations have changed the emphasis to developing, nurturing, supporting, facilitating – and coaching. Currently we are in a state of transition as many people gradually come to grips with new ways of getting the best out of people. The above approach is of the old school. It still has its place but the range of activities and processes now considered as coaching is much wider.

The terms 'trainee', 'subordinate', even 'coachee' are used to describe the person being coached. You will not find them in this

1

book. We prefer to use the term 'the person being coached' For coaching to be fully effective there has to be an adult-to-adult relationship between the coach and the person being coached. It is about developing productive working relationships, not controlling people like children. A parent-to-child relationship prevents one from realising the true power of coaching. This book challenges the role of managers in modern-day society. Some of the concepts and techniques may be uncomfortable for some people and may therefore be dismissed out of hand. However it is our firm belief that they are effective. This belief is not based on theory but on real-life practical case studies. The shift towards coaching as a management style is well under way. As more evidence becomes available of the value of investing scarce time and resources in a coaching approach, so more people will learn the skills. Coaching is not a new fad. It is a new way of working together most productively and effectively in empowering organisations.

This new way of working has been predicted by the futurists for many years. Naisbitt and Aburdene said in the 1970s:

> The dominant principle of organisation has shifted from management (once needed in order to control an enterprise), to leadership (now needed to bring out the best in people and to respond quickly to change) . . . To lead, one must learn to coach, inspire and gain other people's commitment . . . The new workforce of the 1990s will help your company achieve its objectives if it can achieve its own personal objectives as part of the bargain.

It is however only recently that the tide has started to turn significantly towards a coaching approach as 'the way we do things around here'.

Competency development

Coaching, in its management role, is a tool that managers can use to develop their people. In the ever-changing environment of work we are now becoming used to the plethora of new management theories appearing in the market place. Among these theories and initiatives is the use of competencies to assess and develop people in order to maximise both the skills of the individual and the success of the organisation.

To understand coaching better in real terms we must first look at how it fits into the competency framework as an additional developmental tool.

A competency is made up of:

- skills, which tend to be task- and job-specific
- knowledge – what is required to complete the skill to a higher degree
- attitude – the inner feelings and thoughts

All of which are shown through

- behaviour – actions that one sees

The training and development of employees was previously concerned with the first two aspects of a competency, ie skills and knowledge. It has also been the responsibility of the training and personnel function. This in itself has led to opposition from some managers, who do not see the function as having operational credibility. Training professionals have been concerned with the writing and implementation of various training programmes which have, in the main, been in a classroom-based format by which information on 'how to' has been implanted into tired, over-worked management brains.

The area of attitude has been addressed in a similar fashion, with varying degrees of success. But this method of training through 'chalk and talk' may not have a lasting effect. Many experts in customer service look to the theme parks when seeking an example of good practice in the development of the right attitude. But success for these theme parks is achieved through intensive training and a culture that dictates the behaviours of its employees. It is not so much a training initiative that creates the sparkling attitude of staff and the explosive, exciting atmosphere, but a culture that ensures that all employees are fully aware of the organisation's expectations, and systems that are designed to monitor and evaluate performance rigidly. It is common for service industries to visit such places of 'excellence' with a view to recreating the same attitude and atmosphere in their own establishments by using training programmes alone. Many are disappointed with the results.

Coaching within a competency framework enables individuals rather than dictates to them. Attitudes and behaviour can only be changed or modified by the individual concerned. They must own and accept their current behaviour in order to have the will to move to other ways of behaving.

By using coaching, people are able to see for themselves those areas of development relevant to them. It also provides an excellent tool to develop the whole competency rather than just one or two areas.

Definitions of coaching

The simplest definition of coaching is 'bringing out the best in people'. However, the term means different things to different people. Try asking some of your colleagues for their definition. You will usually find such terms as developing skills, giving support and encouragement, guidance, passing on knowledge and expertise, and personal development in their answers.

There are different levels of understanding about coaching. Use the following list to find out what different people mean when they use the term.

Different understandings of coaching

- **skills transfer through one-to-one training** – passing on specific skills to another person, such as how to use a chip fryer
- **grooming** – preparing others for promotion or interview
- **correcting performance** – working on improving a particular area of performance that does not meet the required standard
- **rehearsal** – running through a presentation before delivery and giving feedback on improvements to be made
- **problem-solving** – helping someone to solve a particular problem where they are stuck
- **development of poor performers** – remedial work with an individual whose overall performance is poor
- **working on task performance** – helping someone to carry out the activities required to complete a particular task that he or she may be unfamiliar with

- **telling others how to do something** – instructing someone on how you want a particular task done

There are other variations on the theme but this list should help you discover what others mean when they use the term 'coaching'. If you want to encourage coaching in your organisation it will help if you have some common understanding about the use of the word.

For a lot of people, coaching is specifically about improving people's skills so that they can peform better. There is a sense of creating improvement by transferring some of the skills, knowledge and expertise of the coach to the person being coached. The implication is that the coach must have some knowledge and ability that they can transfer to the other person. For example, to coach rather than instruct someone in developing computer skills you need to be able to use a computer yourself. Here coaching is about transferring your skills in such a way that the learner can receive hands-on experience and guidance. But this assumes that you cannot coach in areas where you may not know more about the subject than the other person. How many times, for example, have you heard a manager say, 'I wouldn't ask my staff to do anything that I couldn't do'? Yet with the ever-increasing pace of change, they cannot possibly keep abreast of all the latest developments that their staff need to know about. Here we come to another point about coaching. It involves letting go of too much control.

Coaching for skills improvement does work, particularly with new recruits eager to learn. However, it still implies that there is a lot of input from the coach and that the other person is being told what to do – and guess who's in control!

At the other end of what we might call the coaching spectrum (see Figure 1.1) is the coach who is able to bring about significant improvements in performance through coming at coaching from a developmental angle. It is more about 'pulling out' than 'putting in'. There is less telling and more asking. To check where you are on the coaching spectrum, check who does most of the talking – you or the person being coached.

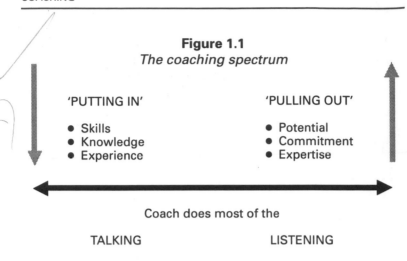

Figure 1.1
The coaching spectrum

'PUTTING IN'   'PULLING OUT'

● Skills   ● Potential
● Knowledge   ● Commitment
● Experience   ● Expertise

Coach does most of the

TALKING   LISTENING

Figure 1.2 gives two definitions of coaching, one at each end of the spectrum.

Figure 1.2
Two definitions of coaching

MANAGEMENT   ACHIEVEMENT
COACHING   COACHING

A process by which a manager, through discussion and guided activity, helps a member of staff to solve a problem or carry out a task better. The focus is on practical improvement of performance and development of specific skills

A continuous and participative process whereby the coach provides both the opportunity and the encouragement for an individual to address his or her needs effectively in the context of personal and organisational objectives

Our experience is that if you approach coaching from the achivement coaching end of the spectrum the people you are coaching will be much more receptive to skills and competency development. You will get results faster and gain commitment by focusing on the individual's needs and objectives rather than just your own or the organisation's.

This approach also helps to overcome one of the most common barriers to coaching – a fear of having less knowledge than the other person. In fast-moving environments managers' skills and knowledge can quickly be overtaken by those of their specialist staff. You can coach without needing expert knowledge of a subject using the achievement coaching process – you do not need to be an expert in everything!

Methods often mistaken for coaching

Counselling

One definition of counselling is 'the provision of opportunities for the client to explore, discover and clarify ways of living more resourcefully and towards greater well-being'. Unfortunately, during the 1980s counselling was seen in business as a method to be used for employees who were not performing to the standards required. It was in many instances never fully accepted by operational management.

Counselling encourages managers to listen actively to their direct reports, to use questions to establish the facts and to allow the individual to reach a suitable outcome. Often the manager will offer encouragement along the lines of 'I can understand your concern' or 'I'm sure there is a way around this.' It is seen as a method to use when problems surface or as an option enforced by the company's discipline procedure! In some organisations employees are required to attend a counselling interview with their manager if they are late for work more than a certain number of times. Going for counselling has come to be seen as a punishment for incorrect behaviour.

Today you will find many managers who have been trained in such methods seeing coaching as another term for counselling. But as we have seen, counselling is normally problem-based whereas coaching is about future opportunities. The light dawned in the eyes of an operations director we talked to who suddenly said, 'Yes – there doesn't have to be anything wrong with you to be coached!' He had identified one of the key differences between coaching and counselling. Coaching is opportunity-focused whereas counselling is problem-based. That is not to say that there are no areas of overlap. There are, and the skills required are very similar. Coaching cannot take place when someone is in the depths of despair or in a very negative state. This is an area where counselling is more appropriate. Only experience can show you such areas of overlap and situations where other supportive interventions may be more effective.

Figure 1.3 demonstrates the key difference between coaching and counselling. Coaching takes place primarily in the top right-hand corner, focusing on future opportunities. Counselling starts in the bottom left-hand corner, concerned with past problems.

Figure 1.3
The difference between coaching and counselling

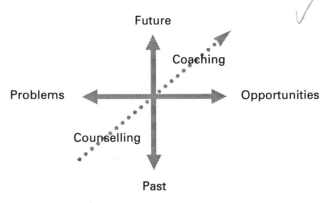

In order to avoid becoming too idealistic, coaching has to take account of possible future problems. It may also start from a problem rather than a future opportunity. At a workshop on coaching, participants were asked to come up with a coaching plan for one of their staff. Out of the 16 people present only two took a future opportunity as the basis for coaching. All the others were based on a past or current problem!

Training

Confusion also arises out of the training concept. Managers see coaching as getting someone to do something better; it has even been linked to sports coaching. Although it is seen as being much softer than the traditional approach towards training, employees are still being coached in order to complete a particular task successfully. The areas within the competency framework being addressed are skills and knowledge, whereas attitude and behaviour are often omitted.

Corrective coaching in a one-to-one training situation is also often mistaken for coaching in its true sense. When discussing the coaching process with a manager in the insurance services industry he said, 'Oh, yes I know about this coaching stuff, I've been on a course. It was very good, and I have no problems now when I have to correct staff who are not working to standard.'

Corrective coaching occurs when a fault is identified by the manager. If a training need is identified, then the employee is retrained in the aspect of the task not being performed to the required standard. The individual is normally questioned to establish that there is a fault in the completion of the task, and to gain their commitment to ensuring that it does not happen again. A short one-to-one training session in the relevant area follows, often accompanied by the threat that he or she may make a mistake once, but not twice.

In the hotel and catering industry corrective coaching has been included in on-the-job 'train the trainer' courses for many years and because of this link many managers in the industry who have gained the training award see coaching as a corrective process. Companies in this area wishing to introduce achievement or management coaching have come up against a barrier in understanding because of this.

'Sitting with Nellie'

This is another approach which is often confused with coaching. It involves sitting new recruits alongside an experienced worker, and is highly successful so long as those involved in the delivery are themselves trained in how to pass on information and have suitable training aids and tools. Where there are no tools available to assist with the training the new recruits will pick up the trainer's ('Nellie's') standards for the job, which may not be those required by the organisation.

At its best, this approach can enable new employees to feel comfortable in their new position while learning the required standards. At its worst, the new employee will be at a total loss because 'Nellie' is unable to train or communicate effectively.

Mentoring

Mentoring has been defined as 'providing individuals with the opportunity, through regular discussion, to look objectively at their performance and future development. Mentors should also be able to share a broad awareness of the organisation's business and their profession's opportunities.'

It is a process whereby a more experienced manager assists in the development of a junior member of staff from another area of the organisation. In formalised mentoring programmes it is not normally the line manager who acts as mentor but another senior manager in the organisation. Mentoring is usually focused on career development opportunities for the younger person and is actively encouraged by some professional institutions.

Mentoring has been used very successfully in some organisations, and it is often confused with coaching. That is not to say that mentors do not use coaching techniques. However mentoring is used to assist young managers to become familiar with the political and management systems used in the organisation. It encourages young managers to base their performance on a senior manager and can be flawed in that it does not always encourage them to release enough of their own potential, which achievement coaching is bound to do.

Mentoring is becoming more widely used in graduate recruitment programmes. A research project on recruiting, training and retaining new graduates published in 1994 identified several different approaches to mentoring in the companies researched. These varied from using mentors to smooth the way for the induction of new recruits to acting as an anchor person during initial training. Mentoring was also used to assist in the process of achieving professional status and was also often carried out on an informal basis, with new recruits being adopted by managers higher up the company with whom they developed a strong and beneficial relationship.

Mentoring will ensure that the methods, systems, processes and practices used in the organisation will be continued. It does not necessarily encourage change, development or growth.

The strategic role of coaching

With more and more organisations seeing the HR function as being involved with the operational strategy of the business, coaching is appearing as a regular topic of discussion in the boardroom. It is essential, if companies wish to keep ahead of their competitors, that there is a strategy for continuous, constant improvement in terms of both employee and business development. This will of necessity involve some coaching.

Coaching is primarily about listening to what is being said and then asking the right follow-up questions. It need not be just the 'flavour of the month' with the personnel function. If it is it will end up being lost in the 'digestive system' of the organisation with relatively little impact upon its performance. We will be looking at the role of the training and HR professional later but it is clear that operational managers must be involved for any success to be achieved.

Those organisations that implement the coaching process as an everyday approach will be the ones that are seen as the innovators in their field and stand a good chance of growing through the 1990s and into the next century. Why? Because of all the assets of an organisation the one that tends to be most under-utilised is people, and we need to maximise this resource to cope with rapid change. Effective coaching helps make this a reality rather than a platitude.

Achievement coaching

Coaching is primarily a one-to-one activity. It is true that you can coach teams but you first need to be able to coach on an individual basis. Some people are comfortable in groups or teams and find working on a one-to-one basis uncomfortable. You need to be comfortable working on a one-to-one basis if you want to be an effective coach. Like all skills it takes practice to increase your competence and feel comfortable with the coaching process.

There are certainly skills to be mastered in order to coach effectively – mainly listening and questioning skills (the order is deliberate). However, understanding and trusting the coaching

11

process is essential if you are to have real impact.

Achievement coaching is carried out in an environment of trust and honesty. The role of the coach is to encourage the individual to express and commit to action whatever needs to happen in order to achieve his or her personal objectives. It has to start in the current reality as perceived by the individual, but it is focused on future opportunities. It asks the question, 'What has to happen for you to get what you want?'

The personal vision, the goals and objectives, and the balance of life can be explored during an achievement coaching session, using an objective approach. Many people feel uncomfortable about discussing these subjects with their manager, and those organisations which have implemented this process have used an independent coach, either from another department or from outside the organisation. Many people have never considered their personal vision and initially consider the prospect with some scepticism and fear. Once the initial barrier is overcome, however, the results, both for the individual and the organisation, can be impressive.

Possible obstacles or barriers are discussed, together with options to overcome them. Achievement coaching is based on the premiss that ultimately each person knows what is best for him or her and has all the internal resources to achieve what they want. They may not yet have accessed all their internal resources or inner power, and the coach has a role in helping them to discover this for themselves as well as to identify and overcome their limitations.

The mental leap one has to make as a coach is to focus on the other person's wants, not one's own. It requires a significant mental switch to focus your attention on the other person. Another essential part of the process is to gain the person's commitment to action so that coaching does not become just a pleasant conversation. The test of commitment is action and a coach guides the process towards what needs to be done.

Each coaching session should preferably end with a list of actions to be completed before the next one. Check that it is the other person's action list and not your own. It is easy to fall into the trap of telling someone what actions to take (particularly when it is obvious to you what needs to be done). If you fall into that trap, you may well find at a later review that they have not been achieved.

Coaching is a natural process in that most of us have an instinctive ability within us that can be developed to coach others effectively. However this ability may take longer for some to develop than others particularly where the need to control is dominant.

This book contains ideas and techniques based on what has been found to work in a variety of different coaching sessions. It is a practical rather than a theoretical approach and is for those who want to develop their coaching skills to help others. The focus is on the achievement coaching end of the spectrum. We look at it from a developmental perspective which leads to significant performance improvement. That is not to say that other forms of coaching are ineffective but they miss out on the opportunity to win the hearts and minds of people, which is essential to generate behaviours capable of dealing effectively with the ever-increasing pace of change.

A quick guide to coaching

What is coaching?

- It is something we can use in business to improve individual performance.
- It supports competency development.
- It leads to action.
- There is a coaching spectrum from management coaching to achievement coaching, from 'putting in' skills, knowledge and experience to 'pulling out' potential, commitment and expertise.
- Coaching is different from counselling, training and mentoring.
- Coaches have to work from the other person's objectives.
- Coaching is an ongoing process that requires good listening and questioning skills.

2
The Skills of Coaching

Introduction

In order to improve your competence as a coach there are a number of core skills that can be developed. These enhance your ability to coach effectively and are additional skills to develop your own personal coaching style; they are not a mechanical guide to follow.

Listening and questioning are key skills you need to develop, but always in the context of coaching. Coaching is not the same as interrogation or interviewing, and questions are about the future not the past. A common pitfall to avoid as a coach is to spend too much time questioning the other person about the past. You do not have to understand all the background information – remember that you are working from their agenda not your own. There are exercises that you can undertake to improve certain coaching skills, but as with all skills, it is practice that makes perfect. If you have a good rapport with the other person you will be excused the occasional clumsiness. Someone once commented during a coaching session that they had been asked the wrong question. They told the coach which question they should have been asked, and the conversation carried on from there.

In this chapter we will outline the core skills that we have observed are used by effective coaches. We have also devised a self-assessment questionnaire for you to complete to help you indentify skills you want to improve. A variety of skills is needed to ensure that you are an effective coach, and training in this area is important. But it is not enough to focus purely on a skills set. These skills have to be put into a coaching context to be effective in realising people's potential.

Coaching skills in context

Newcomers to coaching often comment on their discomfort with the process. Listening and asking questions in coaching mode means that the other person does most of the talking. Some coaches initially feel uncomfortable, fearing that they have not given enough input. Yet surprisingly the other person may thank you profusely for all the help that you have given them. While you may be thinking, 'But I haven't done anything', they will have gained a lot from your undivided attention. One test of effective coaching is the response from the other person, so accept their feedback with gratitude.

Coaching may not be your natural way of operating, particularly if you are used to telling people what to do, so in order to get into 'coaching mode' you may find it useful to imagine putting on a baseball hat with the word 'coach' emblazoned across it! But it is important to be yourself when you have your coaching hat on. Do not try to be someone else or put on an act, because the other person will see right through you. You also do not have to adopt the hushed conciliatory tones or penetrating gaze of some counsellors. Coaching is not a 'tell me all your problems and now feel better session'. It is an adult conversation where you are giving your time and energy for that time to 'get alongside' the other person and work from their agenda. You are focusing your attention on them.

It helps to keep a clear mind and put your own intruding thoughts to one side. Putting your own ego to one side is also important; you are not there for you, but for them. Someone once described it as the difference between being interesting and being interested in the other person.

Some of the skills of a coach are similar to those of a counsellor, mentor or interviewer. It is the context that is different as well as some of the connotations that those previous labels imply. Some coaches initially fear that they need to be psychologists or have had psychiatric training. Rest assured – you do not need that depth of knowledge to be a skilled coach; it may even be a hindrance. One of the areas we have discovered from the people we have coached is that they have never felt that we were trying to label them against some form of psychological model or personality type or to put them under a microscope. Coaching is a non-threatening, non-invasive process; we do not go in for deep, probing questions. It is safe, and you will not harm the other person if you follow the basic principles, namely, working from their agenda and remembering that they know what is best for them and have all the internal resources to achieve what they want. Coaching is an interdependent relationship: the other person is not solely dependent upon you.

Basic skills as a prelude to coaching

Get yourself comfortable before you engage in a coaching dialogue by thinking through your opening words and sitting or standing comfortably. The important thing is to look comfortable, even if you do not initially feel so. Open a dialogue in conversational tones and with relaxed body language. Put away your interview pad and look at the other person rather than at your notes. Maintain occasional eye contact and let your eyes wander gently over the other person but do not stare. Be responsive – smile, nod or grunt occasionally.

Body language

It may be useful to look at some of the basics of body language here. You need to be aware of your own body language and that of others; research indicates that over half of communication between people is non-verbal. When seated, sit either opposite or to one side of the other person. Sit in an open position with your arms uncrossed and your body turned towards them. If you cross your legs, cross them towards them. Try not to clench your hands or tap your feet – relax! Feel free to move around in your chair and avoid adopting a rigid, fixed body posture. You must not drop into a set, immobile position or you may come across as icy. Leave your pen alone and do not point it at the other person. If you are standing, stand in front of them or slightly to one side. Do not get so close that you invade their personal space. Show that you are listening by nodding occasionally and inclining your head towards them but do not overdo it or you will fall into the 'nodding dog' syndrome.

Having got your own body language right, what about that of the other person? You can gain a great deal of information about others by paying attention to their body language. In coaching this is principally about the congruency between the words spoken and the accompanying body posture. How do people sit when they are motivated, passionate and committed to a particular course of action? Normally they will sit upright, leaning forward slightly, head up and bright-eyed. When people are depressed, demotivated or disillusioned they will probably sit back or slouched, arms folded, head down. As a coach you can influence their body language by your own. At times you may need to become animated in order to animate them. At other times you may need to adopt a more relaxed and quieter body posture to slow them down.

A lot has been written about how to read other people's thoughts through their gestures. It is useful to be aware of the sorts of things that we do when we are uncomfortable about what we are saying. The way you use this information is important. You should use it to support the other person by asking appropriate questions at the appropriate time – not 'I've noticed that you just scratched your nose and rubbed the back of your neck – you must be lying!' rather 'How do you feel about that?' or 'Is that something you really want to do?'

One way of remembering the sorts of things that people do when they are uncomfortable is the picture of the three monkeys – 'Hear no evil, see no evil, speak no evil.' It is based on the observation that if someone does not like the sound of what is being said they tend to scratch their ears, poke them or fold their ears over. If they do not like the look of things you may notice them rubbing their eyes or fiddling with their glasses. And if they do not like what they are saying, or feel uncomfortable with the words that they are using, they may cover their mouths, scratch their lips or rub their nose. The golden rule for observers of body language is to notice clusters of gestures and not read too much into an isolated scratch of the nose. After all, they may just have an itchy nose!

When coaching, pay attention both to your own body language and that of the other person. You are aiming to achieve a relaxed state so that you can coach effectively. But do not overdo it. If you focus your attention entirely on interpreting their body language you will become an observer instead of a coach.

Remember that as with any new skill we learn, it takes time before it becomes effortless. A useful model that acknowledges this is the move from unconscious incompetence to eventual conscious competence (see Figure 2.1).

17

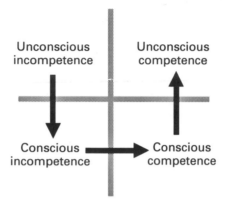

Figure 2.1
Becoming competent in new skills

It is a bit like learning to drive a car. In our infant years we were unconsciously incompetent at driving. Once we had our first lesson we realised consciously how incompetent we were. As we had more lessons we then moved into a state of conscious competence as we carefully manoeuvred our way around round-abouts. Experienced drivers then move to a state of unconscious competence where the unconscious part of the brain takes care of the mechanics of driving, while the conscious brain thinks of other things. In a similar way with coaching, it may initially feel uncomfortable as we work our way through the consciously incompetent stage. Practice will make it more comfortable. Trust the process!

Specific skills for coaches

Later on we have a self-assessment exercise to help you rate your current competence in coaching skills. However let us first look at what we mean by these skills in a coaching context. The skill of asking questions can mean many things from interrogating, gathering information and checking understanding to exploring the past, probing and leading.

The most important skill in coaching is active listening.

Active listening

Active listening occurs when you open your senses to hear what is being said – and not said – by the other person. Someone once described it as listening to a piece of classical music. You hear the high pitch of the violins, the mellow sounds of the cello and double bass, the piercing shrieks of the trumpets and fruity tones of the saxophones underlain by the percussion. And occasionally you may hear a discord – something in the case of coaching that does not quite ring true.

You know when you have been actively listening to someone for a long period, because your brain starts to ache! Questions will start to form in your mind as a result of what you hear. These are what we call listening questions, but make sure that your are listening rather than busily trying to formulate the next question in your mind. You need to be listening to the tone and pitch of voice as well as the actual words being used. Certain words or phrases may keep appearing that help you get a feel for what the other person is really saying. For example there are some key words to listen for which suggest what the other person is thinking. Two you may notice are: 'I'll *try* to', which implies that they expect to fail; and 'I *should* do so', which implies that they are not really committed or that someone else says they should but they do not really want to. When you are in active listening mode with your coaching hat on you will hear a lot more than you previously imagined. Do not glaze over if your brain becomes overloaded with a lot of words coming at you. Listen to the flow of the words and get a sense of the meaning behind them.

Questioning skills

Coaching questions tend to focus on the future. They are directed at future opportunities and include such questions as 'How do you see yourself doing that?', or 'What will be the benefits of that course of action?' Of course you will also talk about the past and the present but your aim is to encourage exploration of the future and actions that need to be taken. You may find initially that you spend some time talking about past events and recollecting what has happened. But by using questions directed at future opportunities you will gradually move forward. Do not rush, because you will need to go at their pace initially without railroading them and appearing to be insensitive.

But where do the questions come from? Most will appear naturally as you listen intently to what the other person is saying. Trust the process and questions will surface quite naturally in your mind. Here are some future opportunity questions that you can ask:

- How do you see yourself achieving that?
- What would you like to do?
- When do you think that will be completed?
- How do you see that working?
- What resources will you need?
- Who else will you be working with on this?
- How could you do that better next time?
- What would completion look like?
- How do you think you can make this happen?
- Where do you plan to do this?
- What options will you have?

Notice that they are all 'open' questions starting with 'who', 'what', 'where', 'how' and 'when'. Avoid 'closed' questions that lead to a yes/no answer and can appear interrogative. Also avoid 'why' questions because they can appear judgemental, eg 'Why do you want to do that?' If you need to find out the person's motive for some action, question the purpose, eg 'What is the purpose of that?' This helps the other person clarify the aim for themselves. Above all, though, be sensitive with your questioning – this is not an interrogation or an interview!

Research has shown that communication is influenced more by how we say things than by what we say. In other words our tone of voice and the speed and pitch at which we speak have a major impact on how words are communicated.

When putting your questions, notice your tone of voice. We are not suggesting that you adopt a monotone or a hushed, conciliatory tone, but the way you ask questions will influence the response. Make sure you err on side of the gentle rather than adversarial. Modulate your voice but do it naturally, do not force

+ your

an unnatural tone. Pay attention also to the other person's tone of voice. You may find initially that they are defensive and unconsciously raise their tone of voice or fill the room with noise – what we call the 'boom-boom' effect. They use a great booming voice as a barrier until they enter a more relaxed state and quieten down.

Another valuable skill is knowing when and how to ask *episodic* questions. Occasionally it will seem relevant to elicit more information about past events. A knowledge of critical incidents in a person's life can be of great value to someone seeking to understand them better. Episodic memory contains information that is unique to the individual, stored in episodes. By using precise questions, the coach can access this memory and open up the particular episode about which more information is sought. Each episode has the following properties: time, place, people involved, sequence of events and behaviour – ie what actually happened. The questions you can use to access episodic memory usually begin with, 'when', 'where', 'who' and 'what'. For example:

- When were you working on that project?
- Where were you at the time?
- Who else was with you?
- So, what happened?

By following this process and asking this kind of question the person will recall the episode. But beware of being too interrogative and use the process sparingly; the main focus of coaching is on the future, not the past.

Giving praise and recognition

Research shows that there is a link between recognition, self-esteem and effective performance. People who feel good about themselves produce good results. However it is fair to say that we suffer from a lack of praise and recognition, particularly in the workplace, because we do not know how to give and receive it very well. A senior manager once said, 'I know that it is important to thank and praise my staff but I don't know how to do it effectively. Whenever I try, it is either met with a hollow silence or slight embarrassment.' A colleague also told us that when he first got engaged and introduced his fiancée to his family she found their habit of saying 'Well done' to everything she did quite unnerving. Over time, however, she picked up the habit and found herself using it in her own family, where previously there had been very little exchange of compliments to good effect.

If praise and recognition work why do we not use them more often? The reason is partly cultural and partly due to the domination of hierarchical command and control management styles. But times are changing and an important element in cultivating a personal coaching style is the ability to give praise and recognition.

Some of the thinking on the link between recognition and self-esteem and effective performance uses the idea of 'strokes' – positive things that we can say or do that will have an impact on other people's self-esteem. These may include admiring the presentation of a report, passing comment on the success of a meeting or simply giving someone our time and attention. Negative strokes on the other hand include destructive criticism, sarcasm and being rude or abrupt. These can lead to a loss of self-esteem by the other person and are certainly not part of the coach's repertoire. The praise and recognition you offer in a coaching session must be genuine, but do not hold back from giving it because of embarrassment.

Positive feedback is a very powerful form of recognition and helps to build self-worth. A model to illustrate the point and show how praise, recognition and feedback can help to realise a person's full potential is the version of Johari's Window shown in Figure 2.2.

If you imagine a house with four rooms and four windows, one of the rooms has two windows that both I and others can look into. These are things about me in the public domain, for example that I am a good public speaker. However there may be things about public speaking that are known only to me, for example that I become terribly nervous without showing it. There may also be things known to others, like certain mannerisms I have when speaking, which I will be unaware of until someone shares them with me through feedback. By sharing this I start to access the unknown potential by improving my public speaking.

You may find it easier to give feedback, praise and recognition to some people than to others. Encourage people you are coaching to

Figure 2.2
Johari's Window

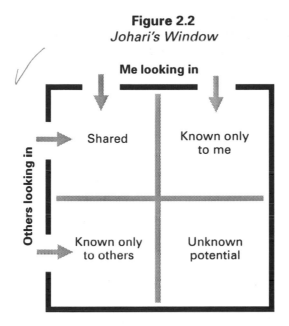

gain more feedback from others through sharing more about themselves. It is usually easier to give feedback to someone who is open to you.

A colleague of ours became interested in sports coaching through his young son's involvement in games. Although he did not think he was particularly good at it, he helped out with some other parents. Then a few of them said how good he was at coaching the children to higher levels of performance. This got him involved with a coaching scheme, and he then later shared with others an idea he had for a sports coaching product. When he received encouragement from them he started his own company to produce the product. It was by receiving positive feedback and sharing ideas with others that he realised his hidden potential.

The best place to start including more praise and recognition in coaching is in reviewing actions. Focus on what has worked well and encourage the person being coached to acknowledge their own success. Generally you will find that people with higher levels of self-esteem and confidence can acknowledge their own successes to themselves and others. You can build self-esteem and confidence by encouraging this process and giving praise and recognition. You may find that people with low self-esteem find it very difficult to accept praise. A low sense of self-worth prevents them from acknowledging their own success. They may put it down to luck, whereas more self-confident high achievers would say that they deserve it.

Building rapport

By matching and mirroring – not mimicking – the other person's behaviour, you can alter your own behaviour so that it is like theirs. When you continue matching and mirroring you may then enter a state that is called rapport. This means not only that the other person has a sense of ease and comfort with you but that they are more responsive and receptive to you. In achieving rapport, concentrate on what you have in common to overcome resistance and distrust. There is a lot of common ground between different people and with practice it is possible to find it. The understanding and sympathy that comes from rapport helps people to take constructive criticism more easily, accept change and put more effort into situations. People in rapport unconsciously pace each other's speed of talking and breathing and mirror their body language. Therefore it is possible quickly to enter a deeper state of rapport by copying the other person's body language and tuning in to his or her speech patterns and the pace at which he or she is doing things. Again, be sensitive to this so that you do not end up mimicking.

Building trust

It takes time to build trust, but it will come as you are seen to be supportive and non-judgemental, and as long as you maintain rapport and give the other person your full attention. As coaching requires commitment from both parties and is not something you 'do' to the other person, trust usually comes quite naturally. As long as the other person does not feel threatened by the process or think that they are having something 'done to them', trust will develop. Be sensitive to confidentiality and remember that some people are more trusting than others. While some will be trusting unless you give them reason not to be, others may be distrustful until you build up their trust. However, as we have said before, trust the coaching process yourself and the trust will come.

Being non-judgemental

Some of us are more judgemental than others. The skill of effective coaching is to put any judgemental tendency to one side. You are there to help the other person commit themselves to decisions and make things happen. Your views on the rights and wrongs of a particular course of action will naturally intrude. The skill is in deciding whether they are going to help or hinder the other person. Are your prejudices, inhibitions, values or thoughts on how you want things to be appropriate?

There is a balance between personal judgement and management judgement. If your view is that a proposed course of action is of no value or potentially damaging you will find it valuable to question its implications or effects. 'If you did that how would it affect the other department?; what implications might that have for the business?' If you help the other person to think it through they may then realise then it is inappropriate. You always have the option, if they insist on pursuing something that patently will not work, to advise or insist that they do not. However, before you do so, check that you are not simply prejudging the issue because that is not how you would have done it. Make sure your coaching does not undermine people's confidence by slipping too easily into judgemental mode.

Being candid and challenging

It is important to be candid and challenging without demotivating the other person. You need to tell the truth as you see it, but you must be in rapport with the other person for it to be effective. Being candid is about speaking out frankly from your more objective position as coach. Your purpose is to draw attention to certain issues for the benefit of the other person. For example it could be that they are avoiding action on a particular subject. A coach, being candid, might say, 'You seem to be avoiding implementing this, what is getting in the way?' But do not labour the point. They know that they are avoiding action and you should be drawing attention to the problem with the aim of finding a solution.

You may also pick up that the person's words are inconsistent with the actions to which they have committed themselves. Just point this out. You may get some self-justification in reply, because we all have the ability to justify our actions or inaction. They know that they are just deceiving themselves. Your job is to draw attention to it and help them identify a solution that normally entails taking action.

You will have to find the right balance between being candid and being too direct. If you are too direct the other person may feel that you are putting them on the spot and they can only wriggle about. The test is, does it help the other person?

Being challenging is a bit more than being candid. It is phrasing your questions so that the other person challenges themselves. It is non-threatening and non-confrontational, yet more powerful than a destructive challenge which may leave them bruised and battered but no further forward. Questions that work in this context include:

- How do you know that?
- What evidence do you have for that?

As with all questions, pay attention to your tone and pitch of voice as you ask them. Gently does it. It has surprised us how much more effective this approach is than the more common adversarial challenge you may encounter in the business world.

Ability to work from other people's agendas

Since most of us tend to work from our own agenda, it can be quite difficult to take as your starting point what the other person wants. Particularly in management coaching, you will have all sorts of pressures on you to achieve results, meet targets, get sales, keep within that budget. However, the skill of coaching is to put these on one side temporarily and start from the other person's agenda. A simple technique to use is called 'suitcasing'. Imagine that all your ideas, thoughts and experiences are packed up in a large suitcase. When going into coaching mode, deliberately put it down to one side of you, firmly shut. This is contrary to what happens in normal everyday conversation, where we usually share the contents of our 'suitcase' with others. For example when someone is discussing a project we may comment on how we dealt with a similar problem. Or when someone is describing a particular situation, such as a place that they have been to, we may relate our experience of that place. In coaching we put our thoughts and comments to one side in case they start to dominate the conversation.

Remember that you are giving your time and attention to the other person, not striving for their attention. But do not be too dogmatic about this. You can open your suitcase at times but take it easy and keep it relevant. There is no doubt that at times you can build empathy with others by sharing a similar experience but if you overdo it you are not coaching! Remember that the other person is interested in their agenda, not yours. The coaching contract here is to work from their agenda and put yours temporarily to one side, without appearing mechanical.

So how do you do it? As the starting point is with the other person, you have to elicit their agenda by asking pertinent questions. You are unlikely to encounter a situation where someone will immediately lay all their cards on the table. You have to build a degree of trust to get close to this. Questions like 'What is your agenda?' do not work particularly well but questions like 'What do you want out of this session?', 'What do you want to achieve?' or 'What is important to you?' will usually produce a useful response. Once you have asked some trigger questions and the other person has started to talk, so long as you are attentive and allow other questions to flow naturally you will start to sense what it is that the other person wants. It may take time, as most people are not used to being asked what they want. It may come as a surprise to them.

Giving encouragement and support

To be an effective coach you need to be seen as encouraging and supportive. As we have seen, part of the skill of coaching is to give praise and recognition. You also need to genuinely encourage the other person and support them in thinking through their commitment to action. You may actually say that you are being supportive, but make sure that your actions match the words. It does not help to say you are there to support them if when they need you, you are too busy or make it clear that they are an unnecessary distraction. This comes back to the congruency of coaching, which is that you have to behave like a coach in thought as well as deed. So giving encouragement and support is primarily about making time for people and actively giving them encouragement as well as being supportive.

Making encouraging noises and statements is all part of effective coaching. Comments like 'Go on, you can do that', or 'Yes, you would be very good at that' make a difference. You will undoubtedly find on occasions that you can see quite clearly that someone is capable of more, yet they cannot always see it for themselves. Part of your role is to encourage them to see what is possible.

There will also be occasions when you cannot see the potential of a particular course of action. As long as the other person can see it, that is what matters. They are the ones who are going to have to take the action, not you. You may be surprised what major achievements come out of a coaching session. Although you may not be totally convinced about some planned improvements, when the actions have been reviewed you may change your mind. This comes back to the core philosophy of coaching, that individuals have all the resources within them to achieve what they want. All they may need is some encouragement and support to assist them in committing to action.

Focusing on future opportunities

For a coach to be successful you need to be skilled at focusing attention on what the other person would like to happen in the future. Your timing has to be right because if they are stuck on a past problem they may not be ready to leap into the future. One exercise you may like to complete is to mark where recent conversations you have had on particular topics or projects fall on Figure 2.3. Were they talking about past problems, future problems, past opportunities or future opportunities? In using this model in workshops to develop managers as coaches, a lot of ticks appeared in the bottom left-hand box. Many conversations are based around past problems. Your skill as a coach is to steer the conversation gradually to the future opportunities.

Figure 2.3
Where are conversations held?

Mark in which area of the model recent conversations have taken place

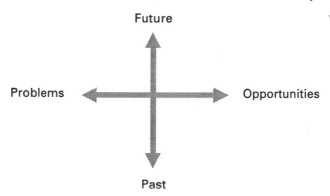

By focusing attention on the future opportunities you also avoid being dragged back into the past or slipping into interrogation mode where your time is spent gathering information about past events. Because your questions are directed towards the future you encourage the other person to think about the future. This make take time and patience, because if it is something that is rarely done they may struggle to think in this way. You may find yourself continually steering the conversation back to the future as it takes them time to switch into 'future think' mode.

Future pacing is a technique to reinforce commitment to a course of action by mentally rehearsing a future scenario. Having got to a point where a commitment to action is achieved you can then pace into the future one step at a time: 'If you did this what would be happening ten days from now – what would you be doing, what would other people be doing and saying?'; 'In a month's time what would be happening?'; 'In three months' time where would you be? Describe events around you.' What you are doing here is not only rehearsing but reinforcing the future course of action. By future pacing you are creating a clear focus on what the future would look like and enabling the other person to start off on the track to achievement.

A major negotiation that required a number of stages in a project to achieve a change to manufacturing patterns in several

European factories was creating a lot of uncertainty for a manager. By focusing on the future and establishing a clear outcome for the project, he was able to imagine his way through the stages he had to follow and what he expected others to do. Three months later the project had been completed to everyone's satisfaction and in the way he had imagined.

Getting to the point

Although the focus in coaching is getting commitment to a particular course of action, it may not happen as quickly as you would like. It may take some time for the other person to 'talk it through'. However, you have to achieve a balance between exploring wider issues and getting to the point. For some people it helps to talk everything through. Others need to be encouraged to get to the point. Short, sharp questioning may be needed at times but err on the side of letting them talk it through, rather than forcing the issue.

In particular, time is needed to think through future actions and if you get to the action plan too quickly you may only be dealing at a superficial level. The skill of coaching is to allow enough time to get a sense of what is going on and then intervene to bring things to a head. Trust the process and trust yourself to know the best time to intervene. You are more likely to have to listen than to intervene and with practice you will find a way of doing this that works effectively. You may need an earlier intervention when you spot that the person is avoiding an issue by quickly moving on. You then need to bring them back to the point you were discussing, because if you do not they will continue to avoid it. Clues to this are things like a change in tone of voice or uncomfortable change of body language.

Observation skills

Observation skills are your ability to collect additional information from the other person. As we have seen, we communicate both verbally and non-verbally through our body language. As a coach, you must observe the whole person. As well as listening intently, notice changes in body language, particularly the facial area. When people are thinking and communicating you will notice that their eyes move in different directions. They tend to look up when they are visualising something or look into the middle distance with an unfocused stare. They tend to look down when they are feeling emotional and you may notice rapid side-to-side eye movements when they are thinking something through. Allow time for them to process information internally and avoid interrupting. You may be surprised how much more eye movement you notice.

You may also notice slight colour changes in the facial area and a tightening of the lips and nose, a raising of the eyebrows, a whole host of different facial movements. Just absorb this information and it will guide you during a coaching session. This does not mean that you need to make a great effort to analyse the significance of an occasional twitch of the eyebrow. What it does mean is that over a period of time you will notice what people do when they are feeling energised and committed and what they do when they are uncertain or confused. Allow your eyes to roam over them because you will pick up information about their state of mind, both consciously and unconsciously. It does not mean staring at them or engaging them in continual direct eye contact; it is a relaxed way of communicating by observing the other person more closely.

Being objective rather than subjective)

Being objective is similar to being non-judgemental. You are consciously standing back from the situation, disassociating yourself from your own emotions, judgements and feelings to give the best possible support. By being objective you are allowing the other person to form their own conclusions without intervening with your subjective judgements. This can be difficult at times, particularly if their proposed courses of action affect your self-interest or go against your value system. However, to be effective as a coach you have to learn to be disinterested during the interaction, otherwise you may slip into instructing mode and impose your own solution. People are unlikely to be as committed to your solution as they are to their own, although you may be surprised how often, if you allow time for them to think things through and review options for action, their conclusion turns out to be very similar to your own. There may also be occasions when the other person does make mistakes but learns how to improve as a result.

The question to ask yourself is 'Am I being objective or am I getting too involved?' Objectivity can be difficult if you hit a topic that sucks you into the process. Being objective means noticing when your own emotions and feelings intrude into the process and putting them to one side if they start to turn into subjective judgements.

Competencies of a coach

Figure 2.4 lists the key competencies of an effective coach. Rate yourself in terms of your current level of competence against each item. Score 1 for a low level of competence to 6 for high.

Figure 2.4
Current level of competence

	Low					High
Active listening	1	2	3	4	5	6
Questioning skills	1	2	3	4	5	6
Giving praise/recognition	1	2	3	4	5	6
Building rapport	1	2	3	4	5	6
Creating trust	1	2	3	4	5	6
Being non-judgemental	1	2	3	4	5	6
Being candid and challenging	1	2	3	4	5	6
Ability to work from other people's agendas	1	2	3	4	5	6
Giving encouragement and support	1	2	3	4	5	6
Focusing on future opportunities	1	2	3	4	5	6
Getting to the point	1	2	3	4	5	6
Observation skills	1	2	3	4	5	6
Being objective	1	2	3	4	5	6

Having completed this as a self-assessment exercise you may want to obtain feedback from others by asking them to complete it for you. Try asking colleagues, your staff or boss, even your partner.

A quick guide to coaching

The skills of coaching

- The skills of a good coach are similar to those of all good communicators. The difference is that you are using them in the context of coaching, not interviewing or interrogating.
- Coaching does not come naturally to everybody but you can learn the skills.
- It takes time and practice to become competent at using coaching skills.
- Notice your own body language and that of the person being coached.
- Listen actively to what they are saying.
- Ask questions directed at future opportunities.
- Give genuine praise and recognition for achievement.
- Build rapport as a prelude to coaching.
- Build trust through coaching.
- Put your personal judgements to one side and remain objective.
- Be candid and challenging in a non-threatening way.
- Work from the other person's agenda.
- Give encouragement and support.

3

How to Coach Effectively

Introduction

You become good at coaching by doing it. For some, coaching is a continuation and improvement of what they are already doing. Supporting others is part of their management style. Those who already adopt a coaching approach generally have one thing in common: they are always looking to improve their own personal performance and find ways of getting the best out of others.

This chapter looks at how to coach others effectively, including colleagues, staff and your own and other people's bosses! Coaching is a relatively simple process, but it is not necessarily easy to do. The basic principles can be understood quite readily on an intellectual basis. The practice is not so easy. When face to face in a coaching situation for the first time, panic may set in as we desperately search for the right things to say. At least that is how it feels for some newcomers to coaching. Participants on coaching skills programmes have reported how inadequate they sometimes felt when engaging in coaching exercises. They had to suppress the overwhelming urge to take charge and start telling the other person what to do. It was only when the other person gave them positive feedback on how useful they had found the process that they started to realise their value. Even then those with a high need for control had to struggle internally with conflicting emotions.

Having acquired the basic skills outlined in Chapter Two, how do you open a coaching conversation or session? It can be either formal or informal. In the spectrum of coaching there are different approaches, depending upon the situation. It could range from a quick chat as you meet in the corridor to a formal progress review session. Most people react well to being coached once they have overcome the initial surprise at having someone dedicate time to them in such a positive manner. Cynicism, distrust, disbelief and scepticism are common barriers in the initial stages of a coaching interaction. These feelings may be based on past experiences of similar situations, such as when they have been called in for a 'quick word' which has turned out to be a reprimand. In cases where the day-to-day operational language is based upon a quick-fire approach, there may be some initial resistance in the transition towards a more supportive questioning style. One senior manager, when talking to his direct report who used a coaching approach, commented on how stimulating he found such conversations. 'You make my brain think and I see things that I would not otherwise have seen,' he said, 'but what is most noticeable is how it continues to work when we have finished our little chats.'

Are such conversations always coaching? Do they concentrate on work alone or include subjects outside work? What about invasion of privacy? These questions and many more will be addressed throughout the book, and as we look at how to coach effectively you will feel more confident in your ability. You will also start to identify scenarios where you could open a coaching conversation. Coaching can become a natural process once you have mastered the skills outlined in Chapter Two, and once you have found your own unique style based on your own personality. Here are some suggestions on how to get started.

Coaching windows

In the workplace you can find a myriad of opportunities to coach both formally and informally. You may like to start with informal situations where you can test the response to coaching questions.

You may have to seek these opportunities out or create them, but unless you work in isolation, it is likely that you will attend meetings during the course of your working week; people will come and ask you different things; you may have input into joint projects or liaise with other people on their day-to-day activities. You will probably speak to others on the telephone, bump into people as you walk through the workplace or meet different people at lunch break times. Notice these oppotunities to engage people in a coaching dialogue and choose the appropriate moment when you sense it is right to act as coach.

Let us first look at those times when coaching can be used in the existing framework and procedures of most organisations, such as appraisals, review systems, recruitment and assessment centres and meetings.

Appraisals

Without doubt one of the occasions that both managers and direct reports fear is the annual review or appraisal. In consultancy projects across a wide range of different organisations the question has often been asked, 'How effective is the appraisal system in your company?' The overwhelming response has been that appraisals are ineffective, poorly conducted and avoided whenever possible by both the appraiser and the appraisee. It is a process that is enforced by the personnel department in some organisations and in most is seen as being a 'personnel' issue rather than an operational requirement. It is often seen as a time when the direct report is told how he or she has done over the past year and what he or she has to do to improve in certain areas. What the direct report has done may not be viewed in the positive and the whole process may be seen as an opportunity to put them straight. There are always those managers who take a more positive approach, but as with most things our brains seem to remember the negative aspects far more easily than the positive.

Traditionally appraisals are used to assess an individual's performance against the previous year's objectives and agree what further development is required. Organisations often spend some time in ensuring that managers are trained in how to carry out effective appraisals (and particularly how to interpret and complete the necessary documentation). But even after such training there are still those managers and employees who see the appraisal as a total waste of time. When asked what the new training manager could do to assist with his development, a senior manager said, 'At my past two appraisals I've asked for, and been told that I need to attend, a time management course. I expect the same thing will happen this year. If you could arrange that for me I would be most grateful, as I don't think it's good for me or the company for it to go into a fourth year.'

So unless the appraisal is linked to the annual pay award system many managers are not interested in spending more than the minimum amount of time on the process. One objection is the time it takes in relation to the benefits gained. Introducing a coaching element to the appraisal process can bring significant advantages. Once the official form has been completed, areas that the appraisee wants to develop can be explored. A regional manager conducting an appraisal of one of his area managers introduced some coaching questions at the end of the appraisal. He found that the 'glass wall' that had dropped between them at the start of the session suddenly lifted as he took a less structured approach. His questions about how else the company could help the area manager to get what he wanted from the job led to a sudden shift in attitude. When asked about the sudden shift and the lifting of the 'glass wall', the area manager responded, 'I felt as though you were judging me at first, and I knew that what we said would be recorded on the form and affect my future career'.

Most if not all organisations have some type of appraisal system and are often far from pleased with the results it achieves or the general process at all. Take time to look at the system in your organisation. How effective is it? How often *should* it take place and how often does it? Who is included in the process? Is it all employees or only management levels? What recorded benefits are there for the company and the employee following the appraisal? How is the information gained used to improve performance? How much time is spent on follow-up by managers?

With the introduction of Investors in People (IIP) many organisations are now extending the appraisal system to all employees, in order to meet criteria laid down by the IIP body. All employees have to show that they have personal development plans which are also linked to the overall business requirements.

So what is missing from most appraisal systems?

- follow-up by the manager in a non-threatening manner
- any contribution by the manager to resolving the difficulties of the direct report
- suggestions for development from the direct report and hence agreement to action
- a method of recording how the direct report will assess their success following any learning taking place
- innovation in addressing methods to meet development needs

How will a coaching approach help correct these deficiencies? As we saw in the example of the regional manager and his area manager, coaching opened up an individual at the end of an appraisal. If the same approach had been adopted at the start there might have been a more honest open dialogue and many more issues could have been covered. This may then have led to areas of improvement being agreed for both parties. Coaching encourages a two-way conversation that is primarily focused on the appraisee's agenda, with the manager assisting the direct report to explore avenues for development and improvement both in terms of the company and the individual. In our opinion it is essential that both parties feel comfortable when conducting an appraisal. By taking a coaching approach both can become more relaxed by asking questions that arise from listening to what has been said rather than questions that are set down on a formal document.

Some of the barriers to appraisal systems could well be overcome by adopting a coaching approach. It also enables managers who are more familiar with a controlling style to take small steps towards a coaching approach. One public-sector manager agreed an ongoing coaching plan with one of his team as a result of his appraisal. 'I was surprised at how easily we both set the plan, and put it down to introducing a coaching dialogue into the appraisal,' he said.

Review systems

With the introduction of IIP in many organisations, regular review systems have been introduced for all employees in order to meet the required criteria. The Management Charter Initiative (MCI), National Vocational Qualifications (NVQs) and Scottish SVQs have also led to more employees becoming familiar with the one-to-one chat centred around them and not the business. These form natural openings for the introduction of coaching, which may be preferable to suddenly applying a system which may seem alien to both the manager and the direct report. The use of personal development planners reflecting the requirements of IIP and MCI have also encouraged coaching conversations. They enable all employees to have responsibility for their own development, encouraging them to record all personal learning and applications in their work. It also supports the development of a culture which encourages a learning organisation.

There are managers who already have what they consider to be a coaching system in place. One manager reported: 'I know what coaching is all about. I have a file for all of my team. We meet at least twice a month formally and once a month on an informal basis. One formal meeting is on a one-to-one basis on operational issues and the other is with the whole team. I find out what the individual is up to in the business and how they are getting along with their priorities. I know all about them.'

He may well think that he knows all about them and from conversations with his team members he definitely knows all there is to know about their activities in the business. But there may be wider issues that could be addressed were he to use an achievement coaching rather than a management coaching style. Nevertheless, meetings such as these create opportunities to introduce more non-directive coaching into the process. For a manager to spend so much valuable time with his direct reports and gain greater commitment to action rather than just lip service must be significantly beneficial to the company's growth and success.

Recruitment and assessment centres

Other less obvious situations where coaching can be introduced include the recruitment process and assessment centres. Imagine being able to coach an interviewee into the realisation that they had in fact applied for a job that would not suit them rather than at the end leaving them to wonder why they were unsuccessful.

One major building society puts a lot of management time and effort into coaching in their graduate recruitment process. They put extra effort into helping those graduates they do not select to plan how they will find opportunities that will best meet their needs. The business rationale is simple. Those recruits who are not selected are prospective customers and they want them to feel good about the business.

Traditionally assessment centres are based on finding out as much as possible about attendees. This may be obtained through the use of management exercises, personality questionnaires, occupational questionnaires, individual presentations, interviews and group discussions. During the feedback session at the end of the process coaching again is a valuable tool to use, especially for internal management assessment when managers may not have come out of the process very well. It is also important to remember that most assessment centres are stressful for the delegates. If a dinner or formal lunch is included the assessors can not only gain a lot of information about the delegates but also reduce some of the stress by using a coaching approach rather than an interrogative style. Introducing open questions and following them with listening questions will encourage participants to show up their good points instead of covering up perceived weaknesses.

Meetings

Meetings, preferably small ones of four to six people, are a good place to practise your coaching skills. Focus on how you can coach other participants to make decisions and commit to action. Ask yourself, 'How can I coach these people effectively to move this meeting on?' Take time to listen carefully to the conversations and the way people are talking. Is the discussion short, sharp and to the point or is it more relaxed and open? Get a sense of the speed and tone of voice and gradually tune yourself in to the conversation. On a corner of your meeting pad draw two lines crossing each other, one horizontal and the other vertical, as in Figure 3.1. Make a mark in the four quarters of the cross indicating whether the different parts of the conversation are about the past or the future, are they opportunities or problems.

See how you can now move the conversations more into the top right hand corner by talking about how things could be in the future. The kind of questions you can ask are:

- How could we achieve that?
- What can be done to make further improvements?
- Who else can we bring on board to help?
- How can we make things better?
- What are we looking to do to move things forward?
- What are we trying to achieve?
- How would that help us?

Figure 3.1

Monitoring meeting conversations

Mark in each quarter of the model where different conversations are taking place

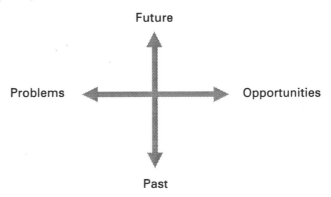

Ease these kinds of questions in at the appropriate moments and be prepared for some silence as others think about the future opportunities. If you are not used to asking these kinds of questions in meetings, ask a few at a time. Otherwise your colleagues may be surprised by your sudden change in behaviour. Experiment with different kinds of questions and notice their effect on others. Also make time in meetings to capture agreed action points before the conversation moves on and query the purpose of certain points. 'What is the purpose of this?' can be a very powerful coaching question when asked in the right way at the right time. Notice how your coaching stance affects the conduct and outcomes of the meetings. You do not have to be the chairperson to adopt a coaching approach, but find a balance between your input as a participant in the meeting and your aim of coaching others into agreed actions.

Mini-meetings

You may find yourself occasionally having small, unstructured meetings with one or two people where you can also adopt a coaching approach. If you focus on the core of the coaching process, which is 'What do you want to achieve?' and 'How are you going to do it?', then a logical place to start the mini-meeting is with the question: What do you want to get out of this meeting?

Establishing a purpose and outcomes for the meeting can be irritating to start with if the focus is on just getting on with the meeting. Taking time to discuss what the purpose and outcomes are may seem to hold things up. But you will discover that investing time at the beginning of the meeting in clarifying these points invariably leads to shorter meetings and helps to keep them on track and avoid major digressions. It may take time to get used to this approach and you may experience some difficulty, but persevere – it gets results.

You may have more than one core purpose for the meeting, and several outcomes. What you are doing here is focusing attention on the reason for spending time in the meeting and clarifying what you hope to achieve as a result of it. Setting outcomes forces you to think through what you want to have at the end of the meeting. The brain takes a short leap into the future to imagine what the best result would look like. Some people find it hard initially to make this mental leap forward but persevere, allow time to think it through and it will come. Once you get used to the process it comes quite easily, allows you to keep on track and review how successful you have been at the end of the meeting. Some examples of purposes and outcomes in relation to mini-meetings are shown in Figure 3.2.

Figure 3.2
Some purposes and outcomes of mini-meetings

Purpose	Outcomes
To review progress on the project and agree next steps	• an agreed action plan of who/what/when
To decide a strategy for this product launch and plan a test campaign	• a written outline of strategy and timescales for implementation • a decision on which media to use and a plan to source suppliers • an outline budget
To start planning the Autumn Conference	• agreed theme and list of potential speakers • suggestions as to other project team members • a list of venues

These mini-meetings do not require copious minutes but they do need action minutes, a simple list of 'what needs to be done', 'by when' and 'who is going to do it'. These can be written on one piece of paper and photocopied immediately at the end of the meeting so that each participant has a list of agreed actions (see Figure 3.3).

Figure 3.3
An example of action minutes

What	By When	Who
Contact suppliers and get quotes	15 May	JLM
Write outline introduction	20 May	FW
Speak to Brenda and agree resources	20 May	JLM
Complete draft proposal	1 June	DR
Place provisional order for space	1 June	FW

Action minutes are best completed as the meeting progresses and then used as a review to complete the meeting along with a review of the initial purpose and outcomes. Have you stuck to the purpose of the meeting and more importantly have you achieved the outcomes you set at the beginning? In this way you are acknowledging your success, reinforcing commitment and leaving the meeting focused on what needs to be done to make things happen.

Responding to requests

If you have situations where other people come and ask you for things take the opportunity to try some coaching questions rather than leaping into an automatic response. If someone drops in to ask for some information for a report that they have to prepare, take the time to enquire about the status of the report and how they are getting on with it. Ask coaching questions such as:

- How's the report coming along?
- What else have you got to do to complete it?
- How will it feel when you've successfully finished it?

These questions need to be asked in a relaxed, unforced manner as you display genuine interest in the work of the other person. What you are doing is putting your own work to one side for the moment and focusing your attention on the other person. It may need a mental switch to come out of your own focus on what you are doing at the time, but seize the opportunity to engage in a coaching dialogue. A colleague was once accused of wasting time by engaging in meaningless discussions with operational staff. It was not part of that company's culture to spend time on anything that did not have a clear task focus. But these seemingly meaningless discussions were in fact coaching conversations which ended with the other person rushing off to get things done. They were not about being nice to people or making them feel better, they were dealing with day-to-day, hard-nosed operational issues that she coached others into resolving by thinking through the problems that they faced, the options that they had and how they were going to address them. Quality coaching conversations lead to action. They may be mistaken by others as just talking shops but the difference is that instead of leading to more talk they lead to action.

Responding to requests in coaching mode is putting the emphasis on the actions that the other person is committed to taking, rather than taking them on board yourself. This does not mean that you do not commit yourself to do anything because you may well do, but the attention is on the other person's commitment to action. If they leave with a clearer picture of what needs to be done they are more likely to achieve than if they leave unclear and uncertain.

Management coaching

The definition of management coaching given in Chapter One referred to it as 'a process by which a manager, through discussion and guided activity, helps a member of staff to solve a problem or carry out a task better. The focus is on practical improvement of performance and development of specific skills.' Management coaching is much more controlled and guided by the manager. It opens up a dialogue that is focused and has a clear purpose. The difficult task for the manager is to refrain from openly taking over and providing the direct report with not only the solution but also the details of how to reach the solution. Management coaching is primarily concerned with improvements that directly affect the success of the business. It always has a process for measuring how effective the agreed activities have been.

Management coaching comprises the following seven steps:

1. Identify the area for improvement.
2. Gain the buy-in of the person concerned.
3. Discuss their options for solutions.
4. Guide them towards the best option.
5. Gain commitment to action.
6. Agree and draw up an action plan.
7. Agree a review date.

Solving a problem means coaching the other person through the stages by encouraging them to think it through. If they are enabled to articulate a range of options which solve the problem and then select ones for action, the level of commitment is generally higher than if a solution is imposed by the manager. Where the manager perceives a problem, it is necessary to raise this awareness in the other person. They may not even initially see it as a problem. Raising awareness is done by asking questions. 'How is that project going?' or 'Where have you got to so far with that report?' will lead to an initial response. This can be followed up with questions about how they feel about progress. By gently leading the discussion the manager can coach the other person into recognising that there is a problem to be dealt with. The emphasis is on the gentle approach which does not threaten or antagonise the other person.

The action plan agreed at the close of the discussion normally follows a standard format. The headings include:

- **What** actions will be taken
- **How** the individual will implement the actions
- **Who** else may be involved
- **When** action will be taken
- **Measures** – what will be different after the actions
- **Review**, when both parties will meet to discuss progress

Figure 3.4
A management coaching action plan

Coaching Action Plan

Topic: [_____]   Date: [_____]

WHAT	HOW

WHO	WHEN	MEASURES

Review Date: [_____]

For many organisations the introduction of management coaching is not seen as too radical a change. As managers can retain some of the controlling influence they are familiar with, it does not appear as a threat to them. They still have some control over the process. Management coaching linked to competency development has proved to be successful in a cross-section of industries as it provides objective data and task completion.

One to one

Once you have taken, or planned, an opportunity to introduce coaching your role is to encourage and support the other person to achieve specific objectives. Most people like talking about themselves and value support and feedback, provided it is done in a constructive and non-threatening manner. Everyone needs to be valued and most people like to know how they are doing.

As we saw in Chapter Two, in order to coach effectively you need to have rapport with the other person. Otherwise you are coaching at arm's length and on a superficial basis. Take time to build rapport and get comfortable with yourself and the other person. Remember that to a large extent you are taking your cues as to what questions to ask from the other person so you need to listen very hard to what they are saying. Let go of the control, put aside your power over the other person and follow the natural flow of the conversation. Do not be surprised if they seem a bit defensive or on their guard at first.

Be comfortable with silence, and allow the other person to think things through. You may be having a fairly innocuous, informal conversation about how things are going, in which case just allow the conversation to develop. Be attentive and supportive. Listening and asking questions is a very powerful process. Some coaching conversations may initially feel a bit stilted as you and the other person get used to the process. They may be quite short at first and need to develop over time as trust is built up.

In a more formal situation you may find it constructive to set a purpose for the meeting, eg 'to see how you are getting on with the project and review progress to date'. This sets out guidelines as to what your conversation will be about but put your coaching hat on and allow it to develop into other areas. Remember, you are not asking them to bare their soul – a fear often expressed by some managers new to coaching.

In our consultancy group we have regular monthly progress reviews which invariably become coaching sessions. They are not limited to purely operational issues. We may start with how things are going and plans for the future but there will usually be some unexpected topic that comes up for discussion. One example was when a consultant expressed concern about her ability to translate ideas into action. Because her high intellect allowed her brain to process information at such speed, her thoughts sometimes overtook her ability to verbalise them, resulting in garbled messages. By discussing the issue she was able to find ways of resolving it to her satisfaction. On another occasion an operational review took an unexpected turn away from the subjects under discussion. It concerned business opportunities in Eastern Europe, and we came to the conclusion that issuing a press release on the subject would raise awareness. Within two hours a draft copy was on the desk – another example of the energy and activity that coaching releases.

In due course, coaching becomes a more natural way to talk to each other. It is not adversarial but a genuine approach to assisting the other person to think things through and decide a particular course of action. In informal day-to-day conversations you will spot many coaching opportunities that you can pick up on as appropriate. There may be occasions when in discussing a project or particular course of action with a direct report, you soon establish what has to be done. Take the conversation a little bit further into how you are going to do it. You are more likely to get positive action if the other person not only knows *what* needs to be done but has thought and talked through at least part of *how* it is to be done. And that is determined by them.

Corridor coaching

It is surprising how many opportunities you will find for coaching in casual encounters in the corridor, in a queue or by the coffee machine. A colleague was recently told by a senior manager, 'Now I know that what I had previously thought were meaningless conversations was effective coaching.' A classic way to open such a conversation is 'How are you getting on?' The normal response may be 'Fine' but with a bit of prompting and genuine concern a coaching conversation can take off. It is not enough to care how others are doing; you have to show you care. You can do this through tone of voice as well as by giving your time and attention. A core theme underlying the coaching process is the establishment of effective working relationships.

In summary, whenever you have a dialogue with another person you have an opportunity to coach. It can be during formal situations, such as appraisals, performance reviews, briefing sessions, recruitment interviews and assessment centres. It can also be on a more informal one-to-one basis, chance encounters or conversations in the corridor.

A quick guide to coaching

How to coach effectively

- You become good at coaching by doing it.
- You can coach almost anyone.
- You have to develop your own coaching style based on your own personality.
- Find existing opportunities for introducing coaching – during meetings, when responding to requests or even in the corridor.
- You need to let go of the urge to control in order to coach effectively.
- Coaching is mainly about listening and asking questions.
- You can have informal as well as formal coaching situations.

4

Coaching Exercises

Introduction

As we said in Chapter Three, the only way to develop effective coaching skills is to practise them. Knowing some of the theory of coaching and rehearsing certain scenarios will help you but eventually you will have to engage in a coaching dialogue with someone else. Start with small steps and keep it simple so that you gradually develop your skills. It may seem uncomfortable at first but with perseverance and practice you will become more comfortable with a coaching style and know when to apply it. Again, it may not be the natural way you currently operate so you will have to think consciously about working in coaching mode. Coaching is unlike normal day-to-day questions because you are working from the other person's agenda, focusing your attention on them, listening carefully to what they are saying, asking questions which prompt and being comfortable with silence while the other person thinks things through. Some of these things you may already do but here we will give them more attention.

This chapter includes a series of exercises and questions that you can use as you spot or create coaching opportunities. You may have heard the term 'windows of opportunity'. We use it here to describe those occasions when you can open a coaching conversation to practise and develop your own coaching style.

Coaching exercises

To help managers to become more comfortable using a coaching style the following exercises can first be completed individually, then tried with a colleague. They are quick exercises that enable you to gain a greater understanding of what a coaching style is like. It may be that as you progress through them you realise that you already use something similar but have not realised it was coaching.

Skills coaching

Every manager at some time or other has the task of developing a direct report's skills in a particular area. These skills may include:

- communication skills
- time management
- planning
- project management
- organisation
- interviewing

The list is almost endless. In each case once the skill has been identified coaching questions can help to reach a mutual plan for improvement.

If, for example, time management is the skill to be improved, the first thing to establish is that you are both talking about the same thing. It is very easy to assume that your understanding of a particular skill is the same as the other person's when in fact they mean something completely different.

What do you mean by time management?

Once you both are clear about the subject matter you can then proceed. You may need to use additional questions to establish what is meant but before moving on it is important that the skill being discussed is the actual problem area.

The next stage in the process is to assess what the individual wants to do better.

What is it you want to improve?

They may not need to look at the whole concept of time management; in fact the problem could lie in another area such as

51

assertiveness. But using coaching questions you enable the individual to explore what the real issues are. Some managers have a desire, once a skill shortage has been identified, to provide a solution there and then. This may be one of the reasons some delegates on training courses find that they are attending the wrong programme altogether.

Once it is clear what the improvements are going to be you must establish what they could do to improve.

How could you improve in this area?

This encourages the individual to come up with their own solution to the problem. A key to successful coaching is to work from the other person's agenda and allow them to find the answers for themselves with some assistance from you.

Now is the time to get some action point agreed.

What are you going to do?

A plan of action can then be agreed. But it helps if they agree some key indicators that will tell them they have changed or improved.

How will you know that you have achieved it?

A simple form like the one in Figure 4.1 can be used to assist with this process and it can also act as a record for future discussions.

Find an opportunity to work through a current skill that you need to develop. Agree with one of your colleagues a skill that they need to improve and coach them through the questions, using the skills coaching form if necessary.

Task cycle coaching

All managers spend part of their time completing certain tasks and there may be particular points at which they get stuck. The task cycle is a simpler version of the coaching cycle (see Figure

5.8, Chapter 5), which is extremely useful for the first-time coach. Work through the cycle on one of your current tasks. Then coach a colleague through the cycle as a way of reviewing progress on a particular task.

Figure 4.1
A skills coaching form

Skill to be improved:

What do you mean by . . . ?

What is it you want to improve?

How could you improve in this area?

What are you going to do?

How will you know that you have achieved it?

Review date:

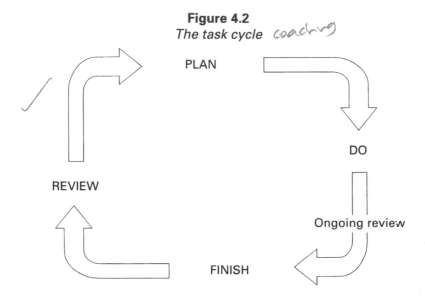

Figure 4.2
The task cycle coaching

The questions to ask are:

- Where are you on the cycle?
- What are the next steps?
- What are you aiming at as a finish point?
- What might get in your way?

Feel free to ask different questions and experiment with open questions beginning with 'who', 'what', 'how', 'where' and 'when'. The important thing is to get the other person to tell you where they see themselves on the cycle. Avoid any temptation to tell them where you think they are, as you may be jumping to conclusions.

Some thoughts you may like to bear in mind on the different stages of the cycle are:

1. **Plan**. For every task there is some degree of planning required. Initially it may be simply clarifying the purpose. There are those managers who find this stage of the process very difficult as they want to get started once they have been

given the task. Ask yourself if this is something that you do. What are the consequences of rushing into the task? What has happened in the past when you have adopted this approach?

2. **Do**. This is normally where most action-based managers score highly – or think they do. It involves the step-by-step activities required for the completion of the task. Are there times when the task is not finished? What prevented you from achieving success? Do you have a habit of not fully completing things or are there too many things going on at once for you to cope with? During the activity do you allow time for a review to establish your progress to date? It may be that by using regular reviews you can check that you are still doing the right thing. What prevents you from holding a mid-project review?

3. **Finish**. There are those who never actually finish a project. Have all aspects of the task been covered? Is it what was originally planned and agreed or have you deviated from your original outcomes? How often do you allow time to check that the project is completely finished? Does it meet all the required criteria? What do you have to do before you start the next task? All these questions will enable you to assess how well you or your direct report finish a task.

4. **Review**. This is clearly a section of the cycle that is overlooked by some managers. Not only is it important to review during the task but it is helpful to take time once you have finished to review how the task went. In many instances the next task looms above us before we can review the one we have just completed, and the natural inclination is to move on. The importance of a final review is that it allows you time to congratulate people on good work and plan how many difficulties you encountered could be overcome the next time. This means that by implication you are giving yourself praise while at the same time developing a continuous improvement process. How often do you and your direct report do this? How beneficial would it be for you if you did?

Coaching through changes

This exercise will help you to coach others through periods of change. One of the areas where coaching can prove beneficial is in oiling the wheels of change. Helping others to cope with change is a key role for the coaching manager. Using this change model will help accelerate people through the process and enable them to become more productive. A common experience for managers is coping with resistance to change. One senior manager commented on how frustrated he felt when introducing new opportunities to improve business performance. 'It's like pushing water uphill,' he said. 'Although my team usually buy in, their initial resistance is energy-sapping.'

The change model illustrated in Figure 4.3 will help you to identify where individuals are in a cycle of change and what actions to take to coach them through it. Plot each individual on the cycle according to where you perceive they are with some current changes. As a result of your diagnosis, note the appropriate coaching style to use.

Figure 4.3
The cycle of change

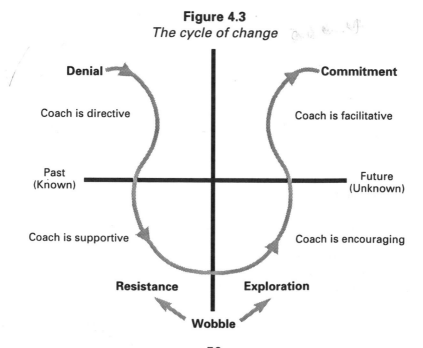

56

Recognising where people are in making a change and knowing what you can do as their coach can be of considerable benefit in managing a situation of change. Changes can range from moving offices to taking on new projects or introducing new systems.

Outlined below are some of the signals usually associated with each stage in the change process, together with some actions you can take in coaching through that particular stage. The mistake that is often made is expecting people to leap from denial to commitment without allowing time for them to go through the stages of resistance and exploration.

Denial stage. It is commonly accepted that most people do not like change. Some thrive on it but a lot of people find it difficult to adapt. The initial reaction to being told that everyone is going to move office is 'Oh no we are not!' or 'I don't believe it!' Some may hope that it will not happen. Some of the signals that may be seen and the actions the coach can take are as follows:

Signals

- apathy, indicated by remarks like 'There is nothing that we can do about it' or 'It doesn't matter what I think.'
- numbness, as though they have gone into a state of shock
- conservatism – the feeling that there is nothing wrong with the way things have always been
- passivity – the tendency to just keep quiet in the hope that it will blow over

Actions

- Confront them with information. Give facts and figures.
- Explain that the change will happen. Keep repeating it.
- Explain what is expected of them.
- Suggest actions that they can take in handling the situation.
- Allow time for them to digest the changes.
- Allow time for people to talk it over.

Resistance stage. As people move out of denial and start to accept that the changes are going to take place they enter the next stage of resistance. Although they may have understood that the changes are going to happen they may feel bad about them and unconsciously resist their implementation. In this stage the coach has to use a supportive style and listen to them as they express their feelings.

Signals

- withdrawal – shutting the world out
- anger or defiance
- avoidance or excuses – failing to deal with the change by getting on with other things
- blaming someone else
- anxiety or depression

Actions

- Listen to them and let them vent their resistance.
- Acknowledge their feelings and show empathy.
- Be encouraging and supportive.
- Avoid telling them that they have got to change or pull themselves together.
- Let them mourn the 'loss'.

Exploration stage. A step change occurs as people start talking about the future rather than the past. It is as though they have suddenly accepted that the changes are going to take place and are now starting to see different ways of dealing with them. There may be some confusion as they explore different options and they may wobble backwards and forwards between exploration and resistance. The coaching style is that of encouragement to support them in finding new ways of doing things.

Signals

- confusion or chaos – uncertainty and indecision about how to proceed
- new ideas – an eagerness to try new ways of doing things
- lack of cohesion – plans not yet fully formed

- experimentation – trying different things, reviewing and amending

Actions

- Set priorities to enable them to focus on key issues.
- Provide support and training if they need new skills.
- Set short-term objectives so that they carry out one step at a time.
- Hold regular planning sessions.

Commitment.   At last there is commitment to the new way of operating. It will take time to get there but not as much time as if you had ignored the various stages and forced them into commitment too early. You may find a token commitment followed by a swing back into resistance. Getting people to move out of resistance when they have bypassed the other stages usually takes a lot longer than coaching them through stage by stage. Projects which were expected to take only a few months to complete have taken several months because the amount of resistance was underestimated. Coaching people in the commitment stage requires a more facilitative approach, providing ongoing support and encouragement.

Signals

- high energy – people are buzzing again
- determination that nothing should stand in their way
- ownership of the new way of doing things
- co-operation
- persuasion – helping others further back in the change cycle to come on board

Actions

- Set longer-term goals building on the progress to date.
- Work on team-building to build greater synergy.
- Reward those responding to change as an incentive for them and others.
- Look to the future and encourage forward planning.

A quick guide to coaching

Coaching exercises

- Develop your own coaching style by practising selected coaching exercises.
- You can develop others' skills through coaching them.
- Look for 'windows of opportunity' to practise coaching exercises.
- Use the task cycle to coach on specific tasks and projects.
- Note the appropriate coaching style to use as people go through different stages of adapting to change.
- Practise coaching exercises first with yourself and then with a colleague.

5

The Achievement Coaching Process

Introduction

Achievement coaching is a process designed to bring out the best in people by focusing on their individual objectives and ensuring that they are on their own personal path to success. It establishes a sense of purpose, encourages creativity and releases personal energy. Participants start to realise more of their true potential by raising awareness of what is possible for them. Motivation is increased by creating an impetus for action.

This approach from the development end of the coaching spectrum is one used by professional coaches. Where an external coach is being used by an organisation there is inevitably a transfer of coaching skills to the people being coached. Achievement coaching has been used with senior managers as a way of enhancing their coaching skills and encouraging them to coach others. By experiencing the achievement coaching process they see the benefits to themselves and this personal gain encourages them to develop their own coaching style in a more effective way than, say, attending a coaching skills course. Once the principles of achievement coaching have been learned by personal experience they can be applied in a situation where a manager is coaching a direct report.

For those who have not experienced the achievement coaching process, it may seem a bit awkward or uncomfortable. Asking someone about their personal vision may seem intrusive or embarrassing and not something to be explored in the workplace. This is a personal judgement that anyone wanting to adopt this process has to make. There is enough flexibility in the stages of achievement coaching outlined to maintain the focus solely on business issues. This may be a more comfortable place to start, but coaching by its very nature is stretching not only for the person being coached but also for the coach. The case studies cited in the final chapter may also help to reassure you that solid results will soon make up for any temporary discomfort, as many well-known organisations have discovered.

The achievement coaching process starts by focusing not on what the business wants out of you and the role you are expected to play, but what you want and how the business can help you to achieve it. It is a mental leap that is necessary in order to generate true commitment to success. It is also a win-win scenario and is based on the principle that if you are stretched and fulfilled through achieving your personal objectives, the business or organisation will undoubtedly benefit. Achievement coaching encourages people to bring the best out of themselves, resulting in higher levels of achievement and success.

This chapter outlines the basic process of achievement coaching, a process which has been tried, tested, built upon and refined over the years. It is a process that has been used by professional coaches in a wide variety of industries, and is also used by internal coaches in a number of organisations. It has proved particularly successful as a means of developing coaching capability in organisations. Coaching managers through the process has developed their skills in coaching others. It is only by experiencing the process that the benefits can be fully appreciated.

Achievement coaching has to be flexible because you are working from the other person's agenda. The basic process is outlined here in a stage-by-stage format, but it is possible to omit some of the stages, depending on the requirements of both parties in the coaching process. You may find that you are geared up to working on a particular subject but the other person is preoccupied with something else. Go with the flow and work from their agenda. There is enough flexibility in the process and your own personal resources to coach effectively. What follows is an overview of the process, with an outline content of each module. Beginners may like to start by coaching a friend or colleague through the process. Even if you stumble through it almost by rote do not worry, because the process is so powerful that the benefits will soon become apparent.

Before we look at the process, here is what some participants have said about the success of individual coaching programmes:

> Since working with an achievement coach I have become more decisive and clearer about options available to me. I feel better

about myself and more relaxed, which means that I am more open and forthright with my management team and staff.

Managing director, service industry

I found that the achievement coaching process has enabled me to be a more rounded person and to take a more objective view of situations as they arise. The encouragement and guidance from my coach has enabled me to deal far better with my team, acknowledging their problems and motivating them more effectively so that they are more productive. The team is now functioning as a much more efficient and cohesive unit.

Sales manager, transport industry

As the start of my coaching programme coincided with a period of organisational change it was very effective in boosting my confidence and helping me achieve goals I had set, despite the surrounding turbulence. Perhaps the most lasting benefit is the one of having built up inner confidence and strength to tackle any problem at any level.

Group training manager, banking industry

What coaching does is to help you explore areas you really feel unsure about. It gives you the ability to climb brick walls.

Business unit manager, computer industry

I've raised my game through greater clarity of thought and purpose. Coaching has enabled me to focus on the important things, step over the irrelevancies – and sleep better!

Managing director, engineering industry

The achievement coaching process has been particularly successful in achieving adaptation to changes such as:

- job transfer and promotions
- product development
- management buyouts
- rapid growth
- business development
- business process
- business process re-engineering
- organisational changes
- life transitions

- company turnarounds
- privatisation
- relocation
- teamworking

Achievement coaching: an overview

Let us remind ourselves of the definition of achievement coaching given in Chapter 1. It is:

> . . . a continuous and participative process, whereby the coach provides both the opportunity and encouragement for an individual to address his or her needs effectively in the context of personal and organisational objectives.

Figure 5.1 gives an overview of the achievement coaching process. Each session covers a stage of the process and should take about two hours. The sessions should be conducted in an environment which is safe from phone calls and interruptions. There are ten sessions in a typical programme, usually conducted once every three or four weeks, although intervals between sessions can be increased or decreased according to the needs of the person being coached. It can therefore take almost a year to complete a full programme.

Alternatively, selected parts from different stages can be used on a more informal basis. You do not have to use every single part of each stage. If you feel uncomfortable with parts of the process, amend it to suit your personal style. However, make sure that what is making you uncomfortable is not simply a little anxiety in asking questions. In practice the person being coached is often more comfortable with the process than the coach. So, if there are areas where you feel out of your depth, keep swimming and go with the flow of the conversation. Working from the other person's agenda provides the safety of not intruding into areas that they do not wish to cover.

Figure 5.1
Steps to achievement

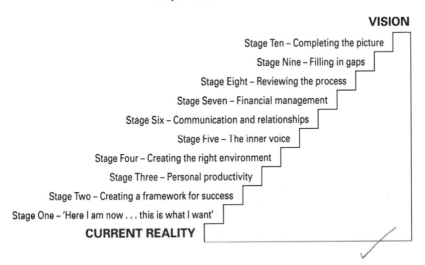

Stage One – 'Here I am now . . . this is what I want'

Purpose
- to know the purpose and overall direction of my life
- to identify what I wish to achieve in my career and life and be in a position to get started

Outcomes
- establishing current reality
- a personal vision
- a statement of life purpose
- agreed success measures

Setting the scene

Use this time to establish a sense of partnership – to let the other person know that your aim is to enable them to clarify and get what they want out of life. It is essential to the success of this process that the person you are coaching fully understands and accepts that this is an opportunity to improve their performance in life and that success is entirely up to them.

This session is the starting point for the achievement coaching process and sets the direction by clarifying personal vision. It creates the backbone to the process by establishing the current reality for the person, ie where they are now, where they want to get to, and what their personal vision is.

Establishing current reality

Establishing the current reality involves identifying where the person is now in terms of career, life, family and friends, even financial success. What does success mean in their terms? In order to help establish current reality one can rate oneself against a set of criteria. Ask the person being coached to rate him or herself on a scale of 1–10 for each of the following headings:

- personal direction
- sense of achievement
- being in control
- physical fitness
- emotional balance
- inner peace
- confidence
- personal organisation
- freedom
- financial success
- inspiration
- creativity

Completing this list will then prompt a conversation around questions like 'What do you mean by a 7/10 for personal direction?' or 'What would a 10/10 be like for you?' You may find that some people find it hard to rate themselves 10/10 for anything, let alone imagine what it would be like. You could have an interesting discussion on this point alone. Part of it may come down to 'not being good enough' or a lack of measures. For example does personal direction mean 'I feel on track' or 'I have clearly mapped out 5- and 10-year goals?' You will find different responses from different people. The point about the list of ratings is that it gives them something to rate themselves against in terms of personal awareness. It is particularly useful when you review progress towards the end of the process and see how the ratings have gone up. We call this increase in ratings the 'magic of coaching', as it never ceases to amaze people how they shoot up over a period of time.

But what is success? We said earlier that it is in the eye of the beholder – in other words success in your terms may not necessarily be the same as in other people's. The best definition we have come across we picked up at a conference many years ago. Someone talking about marketing said: 'Success is the progressive realisation of predetermined goals.' What that means is enjoying achievement on a day-to-day basis, not chasing something on the horizon. We will come back to goal-setting in Stage Two of the process.

In addition to the personal attributes listed above, you can also use the following headings to ascertain how the other person rates him or herself on various aspects of their lives. These headings provoke discussion and enable the other person to establish a broad picture of where they are in each aspect. You will have to do a lot of listening. at this stage

- career
- money
- family/intimate relationships
- friends
- health and appearance
- education and adventure
- home
- fun
- contribution to others

Let the other person define what they mean by the above terms. They are rating themselves so beware of being judgemental.

At the end of this discussion there will be a much clearer picture of the current reality for the person concerned and of areas in which they would like to improve.

Personal vision

What you should be starting to do at this stage is talking through hopes, desires and aspirations for the future. In business, it is fairly common to establish a company vision – 'What do we want this company to look like in the future?' It is not so common to ask similar questions about personal vision: 'What do I want the future to look like for me?'

Explore such questions as 'What things would you like to do?', 'What would you like to achieve?', and 'What would you like to have in the future?' See where the conversation takes you. Prompt questions around the headings we used in establishing current reality. There may be an element of rather vague open-ended dreaming (sometimes called 'blue skying'), but let the conversation flow while staying in touch with reality by recalling the difference between a dream and a vision. A vision is linked to current reality by some form of action to be achieved. You have to do something towards realising your vision and this usually involves action. A dream remains a dream without any action to achieve it.

Remember the power of the achievement coaching process. Not many people get the chance to explore their personal vision with someone else. Most day-to-day conversation seems to be rooted in the past or the present, rather than the future, so enjoy this rare experience. Use visual and feeling words to get a greater sense of vision: 'What would that look like?', 'How would you feel about that?' There is a great deal of untapped potential within all of us and the brain is such a powerful human computer that if you can paint a picture that you really want and that literally turns you on, it is possible to bring all your resources into play to achieve it.

Remember that you are encouraging the other person to express what they truly want. It can sometimes be embarrassing for someone to admit what they truly want, particularly if they have some self-doubt. However, as you gradually focus on what this personal vision is you will be tapping into an incredibly powerful motivator. Notice how energised the other person becomes as they start to see what is possible for them to achieve.

Once you have talked it through, it helps some people to write down their personal vision. Others may like to draw or paint a picture. It does not matter, as long as it is captured in some form. An example of a simple format is shown in Figure 5.2.

Figure 5.2

A format for writing down a personal vision

I See Myself

....
....
....
....

So That

....
....
....
....

Possible Obstacles

....
....
....
....

Actions (what and by when)

....
....
....
....

This format can be used again and again for creating positive statements about the future linkcd to realistic action plans. It focuses on future opportunities, thinks through future problems and relates the vision to a commitment to action. If the vision fades, the written statement serves as a powerful reminder, particularly if the short-term actions are not easy to implement. Figure 5.3 illustrates another 'ABC' approach.

Figure 5.3
An 'ABC' approach to recording someone's personal vision

barriers

A – What do you see yourself as achieving?
B – What possible obstacles do you face?
C – What do you need to commit to action now?

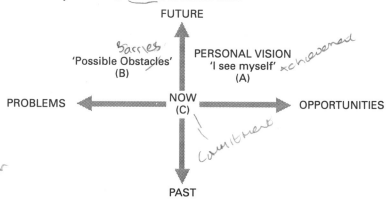

The power of the process is that the motive for action (motivation) comes from deep within the other person and literally propels them into action. However self-limitations may hold them back from achieving to the extent that is possible. We will look at how to overcome such limiting beliefs in Stage Five.

Having established the person's current reality and personal vision, ask them to review their personal vision before the next session to refine it further. Now you can focus on a sense of direction by creating a statement of life purpose.

Life purpose

'Life purpose' means just that – the purpose of the person being coached. It can also be explained in terms of the direction he or she is following. There is power in having a clear sense of direction and feeling on track. There are times when we feel off track – perhaps very busy, but without any sense of real purpose. This part of the process is to establish a statement of purpose. It works by recollecting times when the person being coached *did* feel on track and seeing if there is some common thread. These times of feeling on track are 'golden moments', and establishing a sense of purpose and direction should bring pleasure – the pleasure of more of these moments.

Figure 5.4 shows how by recollecting the past, particularly times when we were deeply moved in a positive manner and felt on track, we can extrapolate that track into the future.

Figure 5.4
Tracking 'golden moments' and extrapolating them into the future

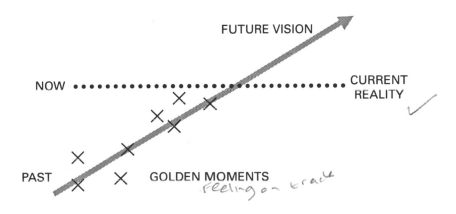

By encouraging the other person to relive past golden moments, a meaningful statement of life purpose can be created, which can be used to check that the person is on track.

Ask the other person to recollect some 'golden moments', not necessarily chronologically. After remembering a few they will start to be in touch with their inner power and build a very strong sense of personal motivation. Once you have worked through several 'golden moments', ask them to complete the following sentence (in writing):

My purpose in life is . . .

Do not worry if it takes time – something will eventually come out. They may need to do some further refining but they will have captured the essence of what their life purpose is about.

Examples of statements of life purpose might be:

71

- My purpose in life is to experience life to the full, enjoy bringing up my family and achieve whatever I set myself to do.
- My purpose in life is to break through with others into the joyful realisation of a shared vision and enjoy the beauty and peace of my surroundings.

Once you have established a statement of life purpose ask the person to check it by recalling instances from the recent past when they were on track with it. Then ask them to keep it somewhere where they can review it easily, such as in their wallet or diary. Recommend that they review it regularly and repeat it to themselves so that they have fully memorised it by the time of your next session. Suggest that they review it first thing in the morning, on the way to work and last thing at night.

Measures of success

The next part of this session is to create some measures against which the other person can judge the success of the achievement coaching process for themselves. Some of these may come from the list used to establish current reality. What they allow you to do is to measure the success of the programme continually. Each time you meet for a coaching session check progress against the measures to see what the current position is. The following is a list of examples of measures of success, but you should let the person being coached find their own, using their own words.

- personal organisation
- relationship with boss
- weight
- achieving goals
- personal relationships
- sales targets
- team spirit
- computer skills

Review these measures at every coaching session on a scale of 1–10 to help keep track of what is important to the other person. Some scores will go up and others will go down. They give you the opportunity to ask, 'So, what happened?', which will prompt a conversation to identify what is working and what is not. You may even find an entire coaching session devoted to reviewing measures of success if there have been some major fluctuations. Remember that a lot will have happened between coaching sessions so do not assume that everything will be as you left it. It is preferable for the coach to keep the score on these measures. If the other person is not aware of what the previous score was, he or she will make a judgement based on the current situation, not a comparison with the past.

To complete this stage ask if there is anything that the person wants to commit him- or herself to before the next session. Ask them to write out an action plan like the one in Figure 5.5.

Figure 5.5
A coaching action plan: Stage One

Action	By when
1. Review personal vision.	
2. Review life purpose and repeat regularly.	
3.	
4.	

Check the actions to see whether they are realistic and achievable in the time-frame set. How can they get a $10/10$ for achievement? Does the action need to be reviewed to ensure that it is realistic or are they setting themselves up to fall short of the target that they have set themselves?

Review

To summarise, by the end of the Stage One, you should have:

• established current reality

- created a personal vision statement
- created a statement of life purpose
- agreed measures of success
- created an action plan of things to be done by the next session

However, do not worry if you have not covered everything. Anything you have not covered can simply be carried forward to the next session.

Stage Two – Creating a framework for success

Purpose
- to establish my lifetime goals
- to create guidelines for my personal success and acknowledge my strengths and skills
- to identify what I need to do to feel stretched·

Outcomes
- a set of specific lifetime goals
- a list of goals for the year ahead
- a list of rules for success

Setting the scene

As in all coaching sessions, spend some time tuning in to the other person and review actions agreed from the last session. Did they get 10/10 for each action? If not, what happened or what got in the way? Take care not to take them to task if they did not achieve all their commitments. The aim is to review what was set against what actually happened. Were the actions unrealistic in the time-scale? Do they need to improve their performance to achieve what they want? Have they added anything to their personal vision and life purpose? Does it all still ring true? Now score the measures of success and note how the scores have changed. Be careful to keep your voice well modulated and non-judgemental. Then show them the scores and discuss those that have gone up and down. Some will have gone up almost as a result of focusing attention on them.

Looking at the actions they have achieved and their successes

Get them to

over the previous period, you can start to get them to draw up a list of personal rules for success. Recall times when things went well and they were successful, and ask them what they did or thought to make things happen. For example if their personal organisation has improved, a rule for success may be 'Plan ahead.' Rules for success are based on what actually happened when things went well, not just how you would like things to happen in the future. It is a way of acknowledging current strengths, skills and attributes and reinforcing them. 'If this is what creates success – do more of it!' All rules for success should be written in the present tense and expressed as positive statements. By capturing them, you can refer to them when planning future actions or use them to create actions when things are not going so well. They are based on the simple principle that if they are what you do when things are going well, then when things are not going so well, you can improve matters by applying them. You can see what the other person is not doing and what needs to be done to get them back on track.

Examples of rules for success include:

eg

- Ask for and accept support.
- Step into the role.
- Hit the critical points.
- Radiate support.
- Break boundaries.
- Have fun with others.
- Get down to business faster

Life goals

This session is the opportunity to review and set goals covering all areas of life. Discuss what the person's concept of goals is. Do they have them already clearly set out? Are they business or personal goals or a mixture of both? Most goals are an expression of something that the person wants to achieve in the future. They generally have to be fairly specific, achievable, realistic and set within a certain timescale. Some goal-setting procedures are quite rigid but we have found that a flexible format based on the other person's interpretation is more successful. There may be some confusion over terminology but as long as you reach a point where they have expressed a goal and are committed to achieve it you are coaching successfully.

Ask them what areas they would like to set goals in. All you want at this stage is to arrive at a category within which they can then set specific goals. You may want to use the following list of goal headings:

- career
- leisure
- financial security
- family
- friends
- health & fitness
- politics
- education

Once you have established their list of goal headings you can get them to set specific lifetime goals under each heading. As a framework within which to work, you may find the <u>SMART</u> process sufficiently flexible to set some powerful goals:

Specific
Measurable
Achievable
Realistic
Time-phased

Work through the headings and ask what specific goals they would like to set under each. Allow time to explore the goal before committing it to writing and setting a timescale.

Examples of lifetime goals

Career
- become Regional Manager   April '95
- obtain national board position with
  £20 million turnover manufacturing
  company   1997
- achive director status   1999

Leisure
- get golf handicap down to 15   June 1996
- visit all the continents of the world   2010
- try a new sport every two years

Financial security
- achieve savings target of £20,000   2000
- set up personal pension   June 1995

Family
- Provide for children's further education   Sept 1998
       Sept 2001
- organise Mum's sixtieth birthday celebration   5 June 1997
- move to a four-bedroomed house   2002

Friends
- get in touch for old school reunion   1997

Health and fitness
- achieve and maintain weight at 13 stone   June 1995
- run a half-marathon   April 1996

Politics
- become Membership Secretary   Feb 1996
- go to National Conference   Oct 1997
- stand for election to council   May 1998

Education
- learn French for holiday use   Sept 1996
- master personal computer for basic
  spreadsheet and wordprocessing   June 1996
- start Open University course   Sept 1998

This list is something that can be added to, amended and altered in the future. To bring goals into more immediate focus, you should now choose which ones to set for the year ahead. Check to see if they are stretching, whether they will require some effort and energy to achieve and are not going to just happen anyway. They can be made even more specific if the time horizon is closer. This gives a clear set of goals for the year ahead that can be referred to as time progresses.

A simple model can be used to diagnose how stretching a particular goal is (see Figure 5.6). High achievers set their goals in the stretch zone and grow as a consequence. There can be another narrow zone between stretch and panic, and that is super stretch. People familiar with public speaking usually experience it when they depart from their prepared text; the brain clicks into overdrive and the speech moves up a gear.

Things that are stretch today will eventually become comfort, so this is a dynamic model which needs reviewing. We need to be stretching ourselves to achieve our goals, but if they are set in the panic zone it can lead to poor performance as our technique collapses and our personal effectiveness goes to pieces.

Figure 5.6
Panic, stretch and comfort zones

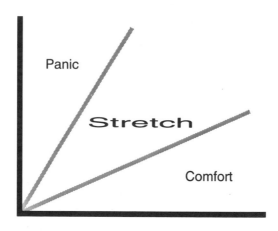

Review the other person's goals against the model so that they can determine whether they fall into the panic, stretch or comfort zones.

Examples of annual goals

Career
- attend assessment centre for internal promotion   12 Feb
- arrange a mentor from Sales Division   20 April

Leisure
- book holidays in Florida   15 Feb
- get golf handicap down to 20   30 Sept

Financial security
- increase monthly savings to £200   1 March

Family
- recontact and visit June and Eric   Easter

Friends
- write to John   Now
- have friends round for dinner   monthly

Health and fitness
- get down to 13 stone 10lb   30 June
- start jogging again, twice weekly   Now

Politics
- help with local elections   May

Education
- buy holiday French language tapes   7 Sept

Now you have coached them into setting goals for the year ahead see which ones they can transfer to their monthly action plan (Figure 5.7) for completion before their next coaching session. Also ask them to review and add to their life goals and suggest that they may like to share them with their partner, if they have one. This can be a very powerful reinforcement for some people and an opportunity to discover previously unknown goals their partner may have.

Ask them if there is anything else that they would like to commit themselves to implementing before the next coaching session. Add these to the action plan and check that they are potentially 10/10 achievements.

Figure 5.7
A coaching action plan: Stage Two

Action	By when
1. Review and add to lifetime goals.	
2. Review goals for the current year.	
3. Share my goals with my partner.	
4. Review and add to my rules for success.	
5.	
6.	

Review

Review your Stage Two coaching session. It should have:

- established a list of personal rules for success
- created a set of lifetime goals
- set goals for the current year
- reviewed measures of success
- created an action plan of things to be done by the next session

Stage Three – Personal productivity

Purpose
- to improve my personal productivity in order to realise my goals and make things happen for me

Outcomes
- a process for moving ideas into action faster
- an increased sense of satisfaction and energy
- a plan for moving current projects forward
- an action plan to clear all outstanding small tasks

The coaching cycle

Ask the person you are coaching for their definition of personal productivity, for example, 'the optimum use of resources to achieve what I want'. You can then outline the basic coaching cycle for highlighting the key aspects of maximising this productivity (see Figure 5.8).

Figure 5.8
The coaching cycle

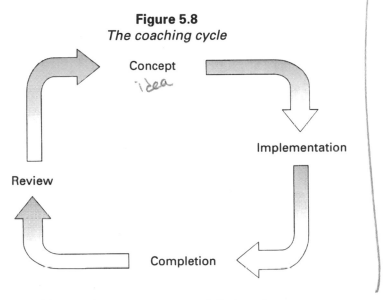

The coaching cycle, as you can see, falls into four stages: concept, implementation, completion and review.

Concept All goals and projects start with an idea. We then go through some form of creative process to work the idea through before making a decision about the resources we will need, its level of priority and our commitment to action. Many goals or projects remain at this stage and fail to be implemented for all sorts of reasons. The coaching cycle allows you to explore these reasons.

You need to look at what the other person does to avoid implementation. What kind of rituals do they use? Is it a short five-minute ritual like going for a cup of coffee, having a chat or telephoning someone, or is it something longer, like continually

putting it at the bottom of the pile? If these rituals can be identified then the person being coached has a choice. They can either
continue with the ritual and realise that they are doing so, or they
can get back on the cycle to achieve their goals.

Implementation This is all about getting down to action.
Ideas that seemed good at the time may become less attractive
once they require action. Some people are good at getting on
with the early stages of implementation, but soon become bored.
Others find it difficult to complete and get stuck when they are
95 per cent through a task, sometimes leaving things unfinished
to avoid being judged or falling short of perfection. Again they
may engage in avoidance rituals which prevent completion.

A common technique for assisting implementation is to break
a project down into small manageable tasks and focusing attention on these rather than the overwhelming size of the whole.
One way of doing this is to get the person being coached to think
through the small steps and decide what stages they are committing to getting 10/10 in by the end of the week or month ahead.
For example is it realistic to set a target of 10/10 for starting to
learn French this week, or would it be better to find out what
options there are – such as buying a book or some tapes, or finding a tutor?

Completion Completion is crossing the *t*s and dotting the *i*s.
It is what needs to happen to get finished and move on. Did the
person being coached set a clear outcome when he or she started
so that you would know when the project was finished, or have
the goalposts moved? Once it is completed does he or she get
stuck in to the next project immediately or does he or she make
time for a review? Most people have several different projects
going on at the same time and are trying to achieve several goals.
However to increase our energy and maximise personal productivity we need to complete the final step of the coaching cycle.

Review Completing the cycle involves a combination of
acknowledging success, reviewing what went well or not so
well, giving and receiving feedback and celebrating successful
completion. The purpose of completing the cycle in this way is
to put more energy into it. It is not uncommon to feel tired and

lack energy at the completion of a project. If you have just completed a long report that you have had difficulty completing within the deadline, it is unlikely that you will immediately feel energised to get on with the next one. Some time is required to recharge the batteries and raise one's motivation. Using our definition of motivation as 'having a motive for action', completing this final stage of the cycle acts as a reminder of the motive by reviewing the stages of the project or goal and remembering the original concept. It also acknowledges the person's success in completion.

Reviewing tasks and projects is an underutilised skill. The pace of the modern world encourages us to move on to the next task in haste and not allow precious time to be wasted going over old ground. However the review process is a vital part of learning and without it valuable lessons can be lost and mistakes repeated. It is particularly useful to review not just what was done but also how it was done. A common coaching question is, 'If you had to do it again, how would you do it differently?'

Review
success
+
failure

Celebration adds the icing to the cake by rewarding successful completion. In coaching you may occasionally ask what is going to be done to celebrate once the other person completed – what reward are they going to give themselves? Because we are motivated by pleasure, having a celebration in mind can help when the going gets tough during implementation. It could be a simple matter of having a celebratory drink after work, going out for a meal or buying some new clothes, but it all helps to reinforce a sense of wellbeing and satisfaction and is not to be underestimated.

Stepping on and off the cycle   Having explained the coaching cycle, you can raise the other person's awareness of the benefits of staying on the cycle and the negative results of continually stepping off. A simple way to do this is to ask them what they think the negative and positive effects are.

Negative effects	Positive effects
• frustration	• motivation
• loss of confidence	• increased confidence
• increased pressure	• better planning
• a feeling of being out of control	• a feeling of being in control

- loss of self-esteem
- tiredness
- reprobation

- higher self-esteem
- more energy
- recognition

The person has a choice about whether they step on or off the cycle, but what this process does is to accentuate the positive and negative effects of doing so. It also reinforces the need to check their commitment before stepping onto the cycle. Thinking through what commitment is required can assist in making better judgements before stepping onto the cycle in a wave of enthusiasm for the idea.

Review of current projects In order to put the theory and concepts of the coaching cycle into action, use the cycle to review all current projects. Ask them to list their current projects and mark where they are on the cycle for each. Let them identify the position on the cycle without prompting because, as with all coaching models, you need to engage them by using it instead of theorising. Once you have established a list of projects and identified their current position on the cycle here are some coaching questions that lead to action:

- What are the next immediate steps to move forward?
- What obstacles might get in the way?
- What would completion look like?

Other questions will follow quite naturally as you explore the overview of the project as well as the immediate next steps. Ensure that these steps are committed to writing so that they can be captured and referred to at the next coaching session.

The person you are coaching has now identified all their major projects, goals and tasks with associated next steps for action. This also creates a sense of energy and feeling of control that is a powerful motivator for staying on the cycle. *big & small (& odd jobs)*

Action plan - review all current projects & how to move forward

Odd jobs

While dealing with personal productivity you can also coach the other person into confronting all the smaller tasks or projects they are involved in which might be draining their personal energy. These 'odd jobs' need doing yet they are continually left to one side. They may only need a short time to do, but seem to take ages, and take a disproportionate amount of energy through non-completion. The worry about them uses more energy than is needed simply to get them out of the way. These odd jobs linger around in the back of the mind, and when they come to the surface they have a negative effect upon our feelings and behaviour. An example is the loose paving slab on the front drive that takes three years to fix. It actually only takes 15 minutes but every time you walk on the drive you think, 'I must fix that slab.'

We can choose to focus our attention on better things. Ask the other person to make a list of 'odd jobs' and then commit themselves to a date by which they can be crossed off the list. You may want to prompt them by giving examples such as a book that has not been returned, an outstanding letter that must be written or a bit of the fence that still needs painting. Getting these out of the way clears the mind and allows us to concentrate on other things. Add these to the action plan (Figure 5.9) with anything else that they want to commit themselves to implementing before the next session.

Figure 5.9
A coaching action plan: Stage Three

Action	By when
1. Progress actions from projects on the coaching cycle.	
2. Complete odd jobs.	
3.	
4.	

Review

In Stage Three you should have:

- established the coaching cycle as a process for moving ideas into action faster and as a way of increasing satisfaction and energy
- created a plan for moving current projects forward
- set up an action plan to clear odd jobs

Stage Four – Creating the right environment

Purpose
- to ensure that the other person's environment supports them
- to create the physical and psychological conditions for maximising their potential

Outcomes
- an assessment of the current status of their environment
- an increased awareness of their personal appearance and actions to improve it

Setting the scene

Use this opportunity to discuss what changes the other person has noticed since clearing odd jobs out of the way and how applying the coaching cycle has improved their personal productivity. Review the action plan from the last coaching session and add any new rules for success. Score the success factors, notice and discuss what has changed and then move on to take them through the coaching support model (Figure 5.10).

Figure 5.10
The coaching support model

EXTERNAL
Resources, environment and actions

INTERNAL
Thoughts
and feelings

SUPPORT
Network

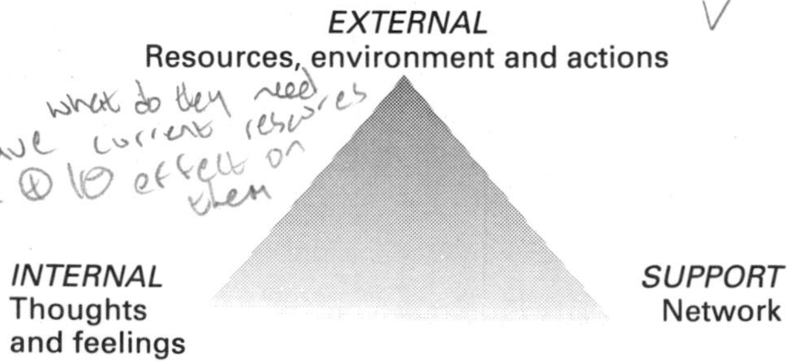

The coaching support model

Explain the model in terms of how an individual can maximise the conditions to support achievement.

1. External   This involves ensuring that all external resources are available, the environment is supportive and responsible action is taken. Has the person got all the things in place that they need to make things happen? This could include tools such as a personal computer, a time-management system, a car, a telephone and office space. If not, what else do they need? Make a list and plan to get them. Does the environment around them support them in achieving actions or does it have a depressing effect? Is the home space and office layout sufficiently neat and tidy or does it confuse their lives?

Ask them to think through the office and home environment and commit themselves to the changes that need to take place to create a more supportive environment. Even minor changes such as getting a new in-tray to sort paperwork, buying a house plant or changing the furniture round can all have beneficial effects on our sense of well-being. We are responsible for taking actions to create the changes we want in our lives.

2. Internal   This means maintaining an accurate and positive internal focus that supports the achievement of action. Check that the other person's internal thoughts and feelings are aligned with actions to be taken. Does their internal dialogue support or undermine them? A positive internal dialogue supports the achievement of action and remembering the coaching cycle and recalling goals and positive vision all help to generate supportive thoughts. We will look at internal belief systems and values in Stage Five.

3. Support   The third part of the model is to look at what needs to happen to ensure that sufficient support is obtained. Ask the person being coached what level of support they currently have and who is in their support network. Examples of the categories of people who can be included in our personal support networks are:

- work colleagues
- parents

- brothers and sisters
- other relatives
- one's boss
- staff
- one's bank manager

Some people quite naturally collect people in their support network but others do not appreciate their value. It is often said that it is not what you know but who you know that counts, so get to know a lot of people! Some people also find it difficult to ask for support and you may need to encourage them to seek it out. The reason for this is that when all three parts of the coaching support model are in place things really start to happen; take any one of them away and they may be making things harder for themselves. Withdraw sufficient external resources, run down the environment and reduce the level of activity, and success will be harder to achieve. Start thinking negatively, undermine yourself and take your attention off what you want to achieve and you may lose energy and inner drive to make things happen. Similarly by cutting yourself off from your support network you may be making it harder for yourself to make things happen. There are many people who will help if asked.

Coaching someone through this coaching support model is a way of checking any areas that could benefit from having more attention paid to them. Key coaching questions to ask are:

- **External:** What is the next step?
- **Internal:** What do you say to yourself?
- **Support:** What support do you need?

∴ action plan

Personal appearance

At this point you can also coach the other person through a review of their personal appearance. Check through the list in Figure 5.11 and see what actions are needed to achieve the improvements in personal appearance they desire.

Add these to the action plan (Figure 5.12) with anything else that they want to commit themselves to carrying out before the next coaching session.

Figure 5.11
Appearance checklist

Check	Personal Rating					
	1	2	3	4	5	6
Weight	☐	☐	☐	☐	☐	☐
Hair	☐	☐	☐	☐	☐	☐
Skin	☐	☐	☐	☐	☐	☐
Nails	☐	☐	☐	☐	☐	☐
Teeth	☐	☐	☐	☐	☐	☐
Nutrition	☐	☐	☐	☐	☐	☐
Body odour	☐	☐	☐	☐	☐	☐
Exercise	☐	☐	☐	☐	☐	☐
Clothes	☐	☐	☐	☐	☐	☐
Shoes	☐	☐	☐	☐	☐	☐

Figure 5.12
A coaching action plan: Stage Four

Action	By when
1. Make changes to my environment – tidy up at home and work. Take action to ensure all external resources are supportive.	
2. Check my internal dialogue. Maintain an accurate and positive internal focus that supports the achievement of action.	
3. Add to my support network and ask for support where needed.	
4. Make improvements to my physical appearance.	
5.	
6.	

Review

To summarise Stage Four, you will have:

- made an assessment of the current status of the other person's environment
- increased their awareness of their personal appearance
- created an action plan to improve their external environment and support network

Stage Five – The inner voice

Purpose
- to compare the person's core values with those of the company or organisation
- to identify limiting beliefs and replace them with positive beliefs and behaviour

Outcomes
- a list of key core values
- positive affirmations to overcome limiting beliefs

Setting the scene

Following on from the session on creating a supportive environment, this session explores in more detail those internal values and beliefs that affect our actions. You can start the discussion by asking how the other person would define values. They can be described as the basis on which we run our lives or organisation. The core within each one of us is made up of a number of values which are our inner rules. We feel uncomfortable when our core values are attacked, and this can lead us to adopt aggressive behaviour.

Personal and organisational values

Ask the person being coached what the core values are of the organisation or company for which they work. One way of doing this is to ask them to imagine a chance meeting with an old friend who asks them, 'What is important to the company you work for?' Give some examples from the following list:

- teamworking
- results orientation
- profitability
- innovativeness
- excellent service
- high productivity
- recognition of success
- quality
- competitiveness
- value for money

[handwritten note: match & mismatch personal & work]

Once they have established what they see as their organisation's values ask them to tick the ones that they personally subscribe to. This will give some idea of how congruent their personal values are with perceived organisational values.

In identifying core personal values, explore what is important to that person in the following areas:

- work
- relationships
- family
- leisure

Ask them to choose a subject area and then elicit their core values by talking about what is most important to them in that area. A simple trigger question that you can ask is: 'What is most important to you about . . .' If work is chosen as the subject area, just ask 'What is most important to you about work?' Let them think about it and they may then give you an answer such as 'Team spirit.' Continue your questioning with, 'What else is important to you about work?' until you have come up with several core values for the subject.

A list of values in the area of work might be:

- team spirit
- security

- belonging
- recognition
- reward
- achievement

You can then work through the list to identify which are the top core values and prioritise them. Ask: 'What is more important to you about work – team spirit or security?' It will take the other person some time to think through the list and compare one against the other, particularly if they are seen as very close in terms of importance or if they feel they cannot have one without the other. Eventually though you will be able to rank them in order of priority. Then as long as the core values at the top of the list are being met they will probably have a sense of satisfaction and achievement.

In order to reinforce these core values, assist the person being coached to identify what has to happen now or in the future to ensure that they stay on track. In work situations check what evidence they need to be sure that their core values are being met. Ask the question: 'What has to happen for you to know that you have . . . ?' For example, if belonging is top of their list you could ask, 'What has to happen at work for you to know that you belong?' Continue to ask the question until you have two or three examples for each of the top three core values. It is important to remain objective and detached at this stage, because although you may have core values in common the evidence you require to know that they are being met may be different. Here are some examples of evidence that a person might need to be sure their core values are being met:

Belonging
- inclusion in management meetings
- sharing report writing
- having tea in their personal mug

Recognition
- thanks for a job well done
- welcoming smiles

Team spirit
- making joint presentations
- shared laughter

Because our core values have such an impact on our behaviour it is important that they are satisfied. A working experience which continually undermines personal values will lead to feelings of anxiety and depression, sickness and absence. Having brought these core values into focus, the person being coached can seek further reinforcement or take action to address areas where things are falling short.

Beliefs and results

What we believe about ourselves and what is or is not possible to achieve affects the results we get. Strong powerful beliefs lead to greater achievement. Poor disempowering beliefs invariably lead to lower achievement. So beliefs condition our thinking and approach. As coach you will start to notice occasions when the other person is limiting him or herself. With your objective stance, you may sense that they are capable of far greater achievement in certain areas, yet they may seem reluctant to take action. It is as if an internal voice is telling them not to do so for some reason. The model in Figure 5.13 illustrates the link between beliefs and results.

Figure 5.13
The link between beliefs and results

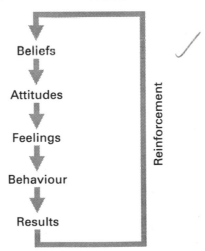

93

If we believe something is possible, we are likely to have a positive attitude towards it. This makes us feel good and motivates us to behave in a way that takes action until we achieve the result we believe is possible. Conversely limiting beliefs lead to limited results. If we do not believe something is possible, we may feel negative about it, which makes us feel bad. Because we do not like feeling bad we avoid behaving in a way that leads to action, and the result is that we fail to achieve. Because of our enormous talent for self-justification, the limiting belief is reinforced by internal dialogue that confirms that we were right all along – 'I didn't believe it would work and I was right!'

You may like to give some examples of instances when limiting beliefs led to limited results. It is interesting to speculate about where these beliefs came from in the first place – were we born with them or are they a result of our environment? The balance of opinion seems to favour the latter.

Someone once explained limiting beliefs as little canaries, issued by other people, that fly around and find their way in through our ears to the brain. Here it is nice and warm and they are fed plenty of birdseed until they grow into big fat canaries. Some of them are remarkably common – here are a few examples:

- You'll never get a management position with a regional accent.
- You're no good at maths.
- You can't do that.
- You are too clever for your own good.

These 'canaries', if taken on board and not refused entry immediately, can build up over a period of years into limiting beliefs. We remember someone saying that at school they kept being told that they were no good at maths because they could not get to grips with algebraic equations. This grew into a limiting belief, so that they avoided dealing with things mathematical. In later life, they became used to dealing with budgets at work, and someone commented on how good they were at financial management. As the figures were always right they must have been good at maths at school!

Ask the person being coached to imagine a humorous character that appears every now and again to whisper these limiting beliefs over their shoulder. Create a nickname for this character, something like Doubting Thomas or the Gnome, and ask them to recall the sorts of things that he says. Write these down on a piece of paper and review them. Are they true or are they just 'canaries' that have been fed plenty of birdseed? Are they supportive and encourage action or do they have a negative effect? It is possible to remove limiting beliefs by creating positive affirmations that are more supportive. Work through the list and see how many limiting beliefs can be converted into positive affirmations. It helps if positive affirmations are stated in the present tense to make them have a stronger impact. Work slowly through them because you are getting the other person to challenge themselves and make choices about what they want to believe.

There may be some deep-rooted unconscious limiting beliefs that temper action, but what we are dealing with are ones that come to the conscious mind. They can be explored in a fairly light-hearted manner by referring to them as utterances of the gnome. Once you have set the process of challenging limiting beliefs in place the other person will take it on board and review future thoughts and how they affect their actions. Examples of some common limiting beliefs and how they can be rephrased as positive affirmations are given below:

Limiting beliefs	Positive affirmations
• You're not creative at all.	• I am a creative person.
• You don't deserve promotion.	• I work hard and earn promotion.
• You are a useless manager.	• I am a good and effective manager.
• You can't sell.	• I am a great salesperson.
• You can't even manage your own money.	• I manage my money to lead a rewarding and fulfilling life.

Most people initially feel a bit clumsy when using affirmations and find that they sound a bit false. It sometimes feels as though the internal dialogue goes: 'Yes you can – oh no you can't, yes you can – oh no you can't.' Not surprisingly, if the limiting beliefs have been whizzing round the brain hundreds of thousands of times it will take a while to replace them with positive affirmations. Suggest to the person you are coaching that they keep a list of affirmations in their wallet, purse or diary so that they can look at them regularly and repeat them at least 10 times daily. They do need repetition to reinforce them so that they start to affect behaviour. Affirmations are a tried and tested process for building powerful beliefs but you have to believe them to get the results you want.

Different parts of 'me'

When coaching you may occasionally hear the comment, 'Part of me wants to do this and part of me wants to do that.' It is as if the person feels pulled in different directions. There is a theory of sub-personalities which states that we sometimes experience internal turmoil because different parts of our personality can be in conflict with each other. It is like being asked to work over the weekend, having promised your mother that you would take her out to Sunday lunch. The 'work' part of you is in conflict with the 'son' part. Similarly you may have promised children that you would take them swimming, only to be invited at short notice to make up a round of golf. The 'parent' part of you experiences inner conflict with the 'sportsperson' part. It is possible to coach someone into getting the right balance between these different parts by using the following exercise.

Draw a large circle or oval on a piece of paper and draw within it a series of smaller circles that house the different parts of the other person, such as parent, spouse, sportsperson, manager, son or daughter, friend, musician, dancer, football fan or social worker (see Figure 5.14).

Once you have established the model, ask which parts are receiving attention now and which are being left out. What actions can be taken to satisfy the parts of you that are feeling neglected? Do you need to do a deal with some of those that are in conflict? For example, you may have had an experience such as driving down the motorway on a bright summer day and catching a glimpse of a group of people enjoying a round of golf. Part of you may immediately say, 'I want to be out there playing golf', but another part of you will say, 'I must get on with my work.' The golfer part of you resents the fact that you always

Figure 5.14
Parts that make up the whole of 'me'

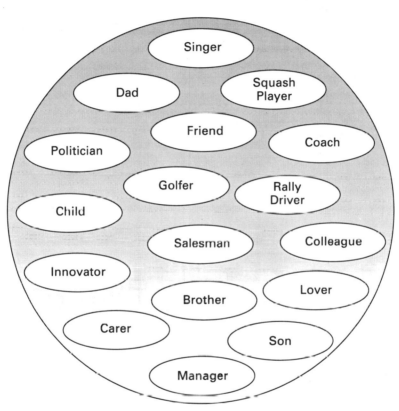

seem to be working and never find time for golf. By finding the time to play occasionally you can satisfy the inner golfer and stop him or her complaining.

Get the person to make commitments to give more time and attention to the parts that need it. Add these to the action plan (Figure 5.15) together with anything else that they want to commit themselves to carrying out before the next coaching session.

Figure 5.15
A coaching action plan – Stage Five

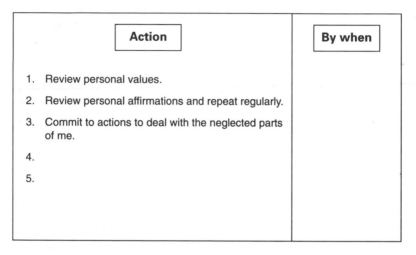

Action	By when
1. Review personal values.	
2. Review personal affirmations and repeat regularly.	
3. Commit to actions to deal with the neglected parts of me.	
4.	
5.	

Review

Review what you have covered in this session:

- a list of company values
- a list of the person's key core values
- positive affirmations

Halfway review

Once you have had five coaching sessions, ask the other person what changes have taken place since they started the programme. Make a note of their answers and acknowledge them and yourself for the success that you have had in helping them to move forward and achieve the successes they want. You will probably find that they have already started to acknowledge what has worked for them through the regular review that precedes each coaching session. This is the power of coaching.

The achievement coaching process is loaded at the start with the focus on personal vision and long term goals. During the first five sessions you are continually focusing on 'What do you want?' and 'What do you need to get there?' As the sessions progress you may find that more and more time is spent on reviewing actions committed to the action plan. You may also find more time being spent on reviewing the measures of success. Where you encounter a significant variance, it is worth spending time finding out what happened. Do not be surprised if you find some sessions devoted entirely to reviewing actions and measures of success. Remember the coaching cycle (Figure 5.8); review is an important part of the process. As coach, you only participate in the concept and review stages. The other person has to do the implementation and completion.

The next five sessions are spent reinforcing the process to ensure that all areas are addressed that support the achievement of this long-term vision.

You may find that the sessions overlap and run into each other and you seem to fall behind the set stages. Do not worry about this, as it is more important to go at the right pace than force progress just to keep up with the manual. If you try to accelerate the process too early you may find that the other person feels 'railroaded'.

In the halfway review you may find the following questions useful:

- What has changed or is different since you started this coaching programme?
- How have you changed?
- What concerns did you have when you started?
- What have you learned about the coaching process that benefits business performance?
- How have you been able to coach others?

Note their answers and acknowledge the progress that has been made.

Stage Six – Communication and relationships

Purpose
- to improve communication and relationships
- to give and receive feedback effectively

Outcome
- a plan to create more effective working relationships

Setting the scene

Review what has happened since the other person started using positive affirmations. What differences have they noticed? How has it affected their inner dialogue and the way that they feel about themselves? Check on the other actions and what has been achieved.

Working relationships

Having worked on our inner dialogue let us now look at our dialogue with others.

We interact with other people on a day-to-day basis. Achieving greater success usually requires the co-operation and support of others. This session looks at how we can improve the communication with our immediate circle of contacts and create more effective working relationships.

All relationships, be they private or work, require effective communication in order to succeed. Ask the person being coached to list the people with whom they work most closely. They may add others who are not close but require good working relationships. Get them to rate the current effectiveness of each relationship on a score of 1–10. Effectiveness is defined here as a mutual ability to get the job done. Review each person on the list and ask the person being coached, 'What can be done to improve the quality of that working relationship?' Specific actions can be recorded as you go along for review at the next coaching session. An example of such a list might be:

Score 1–10	Name	Actions
7	Mary	Sit down together and review exhibition plans.
		Send photocopy of magazine article.
5	Tim	Show more interest in his work.
		Ask him to join project team.
9	Jim	Book to play squash.
3	Frank	Ask if I can help with his new initiative.
		Be more tolerant of our differences.
7	Alison	Give her more notice of deadlines.
		Make time to chat more.

100

The more specific the actions the better. Giving attention to improving the relationship will help it to move forward.

'Indigestible' communications   After eating a meal that is very rich or contains acid foods some people get indigestion. A common comment is, 'I love cucumber but it doesn't love me.' In other words it causes inner pain that lingers. An 'indigestible' communication is very similar. It is something we would like to say but do not say for fear of the consequences. This can eat away at us internally causing chronic indigestion that lingers within us. If we got it off our chest it would clear the air.

Ask the other person if there are any people to whom they would like to say things which they have left unsaid. Identify what needs to be communicated. Get them to tell you what they would like to say to your face, as though you were the person causing the 'indigestion'. Remind them to say what they want to say without fear of the imagined consequences. Write down what is said as precisely as possible. Reverse the roles and repeat what has been said in a neutral tone. After each person on the list ask, 'How do you feel to be on the receiving end of those words?' Take time to modify and alter them and explore how they could be used effectively. Gain commitment as to how and when the person is going to rid themselves of this 'indigestible' communication. Here are some examples of 'indigestible' communications:

- Frank, I found your comments at that meeting very irritating. It made it very difficult for me to contribute my ideas as you kept interrupting.

- Mary, you seem to me to be interfering in that project. It is something that Tim and I have committed ourselves to carry out, yet you still keep asking questions about it that are not your concern.

- Tim, you need to let me know when you change the schedule. It affects the production when you change things without referring to the master schedule.

You may want to coach the person through alternatives to the words selected. As long as you end up with words that the other person is committed to using and that fit with their normal vocabulary, that is more important than perfection. Although they may not use these words exactly, you are gaining their commitment to deal with this 'indigestible' communication. They can now look for the right opportunity to deliver it.

Assertiveness   What is it that prevents people from letting others know how they feel in an assertive manner?

- fear of how the other person will react
- assumptions about what will happen
- negative thoughts about others
- lack of self-confidence

Assertive behaviour is being able to stand up for what you feel is right. It is the ability to give your opinions with confidence and say how you feel without upsetting others. Generally we swing between aggressive and passive behaviour. It may be appropriate to become aggressive when dealing with aggressive people's behaviour, and more passive with passive people. The central balance of the pendulum between aggressive and passive is assertive (see Figure 5.16). Assertive behaviour aims to create an adult-to-adult relationship.

Figure 5.16
The assertion pendulum

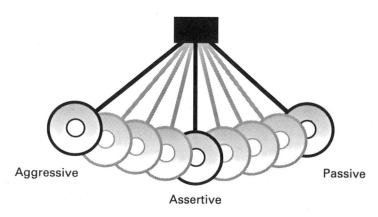

Aggressive   Passive

Assertive

The body language you chose to use also improves the overall effect of assertive behaviour. How often do we say no and nod our head up and down? When saying no, turn your head deliberately towards one shoulder and then across to the other shoulder. This gives a *total* impression of *no* to the other person. As coach, you can demonstrate this and then ask the other person to practise the technique with a real issue that they would like to say no to. Add this to the action plan (Figure 5.17) together with anything else that they want to commit themselves to achieving between now and the next session.

Figure 5.17
A coaching action plan: Stage Six

Action	By when
1. Take actions to improve working relationships.	
2. Deal with indigestible communications.	
3.	
4.	

Review

In the Stage Six session, you have covered:

- a plan of how to improve working relationships
- a process of how to deal with difficult communications

Preparation for next session

In preparation for the next session on financial management, ask the other person to make a list of the following items. It is for their own personal benefit, and they do not have to share the figures with you.

(handwritten: Key List)

- financial assets, eg house, car, jewellery
- debts and outstanding loans eg mortgage, HP arrangements
- monthly income and expenditure

This stage can be left out of the process if the person being coached prefers it.

Stage Seven – Financial management

Purpose
- to review the person's relationship with money so that it fully supports them in realising their purpose

Outcomes
- a list of financial goals
- an increased sense of control over money
- increased satisfaction and ease with money
- affirmations to support their relationship with money

Setting the scene

Explain how this session is aimed at enabling them to look at how they are managing money to support their success. It is not an in-depth financial analysis nor are you going to give them financial advice. It is an opportunity to review their relationship with money. What they think about money? Does it help or hinder them?

Ask them what they have learned from completing the exercise on their personal financial balance sheet. They do not have to show you the figures. Acknowledge their success in managing their money to date.

Financial goals

Discuss what financial goals they would like to set themselves.

What goals do they currently have? Do these tie in with their personal vision and other long-term goals? Are they in comfort or stretch with regard to their current savings arrangements? Do they need to seek financial advice?

Coach them through the next steps they wish to take. These might include:

- Make a will.
- Improve pension arrangements.
- Start a savings scheme.
- Plan savings to meet future, long-term demands, eg a daughter's wedding or house move.

You are giving them the opportunity to review their financial arrangements and make decisions about what they want to improve, but in a coaching environment without the influence of a financial adviser. If they want to seek financial advice, coach them through the options. Do they want to talk to their local bank or building society, or to independent financial advisers? Most people are aware of the options available to them; we are talking about what action they need to take.

Internal beliefs about money

Having looked at the external factors, you can now look at the person's internal beliefs about money. You can ask a series of questions of the other person's beliefs about money designed to help them identify how their inner dialogue supports the achievement of action. 'What do you say to yourself about money?' Ask the following series of questions and note down their response.

- What propaganda do you believe about money?
- What is the truth about money?
- What rules do you have about money?
- What do you feel about money?
- What do you think of rich people?

Review the list of responses to these questions with them. Are some of them limiting beliefs that are inhibiting them from taking action? When reviewing their responses try to establish whether their thoughts or views are

- accurate
- supportive
- disruptive

You may find that they identify some inner dialogue about money that are limiting beliefs. Agree with them which ones they want to convert into positive affirmations. Ask them to visualise what future relationship they would like to have with money. See if they can paint a picture of themselves and money for the future, in which they are happy and fulfilled. Note some of the key words that they use and ask them to create some positive affirmations. Here are a few examples:

- I manage my money to lead a rewarding and fulfilling life.
- I enjoy an easy relationship with money.
- I save regularly to support my future needs.
- I am financially secure.

Add their affirmations about money to their action plan (Figure 5.18) together with any other commitments.

Figure 5.18
A coaching action plan: Stage Seven

Action	By when
1. Complete actions to achieve financial plans.	
2. Review and repeat personal affirmations.	
3.	
4.	

Review

Review what has been covered and achieved in this session:

- a list of financial goals
- affirmations to support the person's relationship with money

Stages Eight to Ten

Purpose
- for the person to complete the programme successfully and fully appreciate how good I am

Outcomes
- an acknowledgement of my achievements
- increased satisfaction and self esteem
- an ongoing support system

By this stage of the achievement coaching process you will be well in tune with how it works for you and the people that you are coaching. It is not a rigid process and needs a flexible approach to suit the different individuals concerned. You may even find that you carry out some of the sessions in a different order. If the person is having communication problems, then do that session when the problem arises rather than keeping rigidly to the model.

These last three stages bring the process around full circle and close the loop. It is important to allow time to fill in any gaps or to cover issues that have not been dealt with. Since the process continues over a period of up to twelve months, the person being coached can take it on board and find what works for them. It is something that they can continue for the rest of their lives. The coaching relationship does not create dependency. By its very nature, it is an interdependent relationship whereby the person can continue to achieve success without the coach continuing to be part of the process.

Stage Eight – Reviewing the process

As in the Halfway Review, ask the other person what changes have taken place since they started the programme. Make a note of their answers and acknowledge them for the success that they have had in moving forward, and for all that you have noticed about their ability to achieve success. Comment on how you have enjoyed working with them and your sense of their inner power and greatness as a person. Ensure that you fully acknowledge them for what they have achieved.

Do not hold back – give them full and fair acknowledgement.

Stage Nine – Filling in gaps

Look over all the person's past action plans. Are there any points that have not been actioned? Are there any points that they would now like to action? Add these to their final action plan. You may well find that actions that are left over from earlier sessions can now be tackled with their new-found inner strength.

Ask more questions to discover any gaps that can still be filled, questions like:

- What, if anything, is incomplete or still feels a bit 'stuck' for you?
- What remains to be done to ensure that your environment supports you?
- Are there any 'indigestible' communications still to be made?
- Are there any odd jobs that still need action?
- What else needs to happen to ensure that all your measures of success are met?

Now go back to the ratings that they gave themselves when they were reviewing current reality. Ask them, without looking at the previous scores that they gave themselves, to reassess themselves on the scale of 1–10 under the following headings.

- personal direction
- sense of achievement

- being in control
- physical fitness
- emotional balance
- inner peace
- confidence
- personal organisation
- freedom
- financial success
- inspiration
- creativity

Note the variation from the scores they gave themselves in the first session. Undoubtedly the majority will have gone up. Acknowledge how the scores have changed for the better and their success in achieving them.

Stage Ten – Completing the picture

This is your final session. Use it to review the other person's personal vision and life purpose. Discuss how on track they feel to achieving their vision. Has it changed significantly since they started the achievement coaching process? Have they pushed the vision out further to create greater stretch?

Talk to them about the value of finding and using support, as they did when they started the coaching programme. Discuss how they can continue to develop their support network to reinforce the momentum that they have created.

Arrange a celebration together to acknowledge the successful completion of the programme. You may want to go out for a by meal together or a celebratory drink – anything at all. an event

The achievement coaching programme is now complete. Well done!

---6---

Barriers to Coaching

Introduction

In this chapter we shall explore some of the barriers to effective coaching, such as organisational structure and culture, the perceived role of managers, and individual resistance to change. Although the organisation may encourage coaching, there may be various systems, procedures and attitudes that sabotage it. The hierarchical nature of organisations, internal politics and fear of losing power, face or knowledge may hinder any attempts to develop a coaching culture.

Barriers to coaching can take the following forms:

- organisational hierarchies
- boardroom resistance
- management style
- management roles
- reward systems
- resistance to transition
- appraisal and review systems

It is important to be aware of the variety of barriers built into organisations that have run on a command and control approach to managing people for many years. These will influence the successful development of coaching capability but gradually have to be overcome in order to succeed.

In theory, most management teams and boards of directors would agree that coaching should be developed within their organisation. They may even be prepared to give their formal commitment to developing coaching capability. But commitment is not enough; it has to be followed by congruent, supporting behaviours and a starting place is with the board. Do board members support each other and coach each other as a model to the rest of the organisation, or is it more usually an adversarial relationship?

110

It has frequently been argued that culture change has to be driven from the top, but it is still possible to develop a coaching capability without relying on a top-down process. Where operational demands require a coaching style to get results, it will develop. One multinational corporation found that some of their manufacturing divisions had developed a coaching approach within the factories to improve productivity, despite the strong command and control operating style of their head office.

In addition to organisational barriers there are individual ones. A fear of getting too close to people or opening the proverbial 'can of worms' can inhibit coaching, so these concerns need to be explored and satisfied. A lack of coaching skill and – commonest of all – lack of time (meaning lack of *making* time) can also act as barriers. The adoption of a more coaching style by managers may also be difficult if they have poor relationships with direct reports.

But perhaps the biggest barrier to overcome is the lack of role models. Where is effective coaching taking place in your organisation and what evidence do you have that it works? Organisational cultures based on a command and control approach do not generally provide obvious models of good practice in using a coaching style. If there is a lack of role models then who do you emulate?

The purpose of this book is to provide an insight into the practical aspects of coaching that *can* be modelled. This may require different behaviours, but flatter organisational structures, the empowerment of those closest to the customers and the emphasis on quality necessitate the development of coaching capability to get the best out of people. Without it a lot of other changes in the organisation will fail or take much longer to implement than originally envisaged. Could coaching be the missing link that will dissolve some of the barriers to the success of the organisation? Is it the missing piece of the jigsaw which will help the whole picture fall into place? Let us look at some of the barriers to developing coaching capability in more detail.

Organisational hierarchies

If the key role of the manager is to coach and assist in the development of their staff, as we are suggesting, then invariably the coach will be further up the organisational hierarchy than the person being coached. The process may be hindered by direct reports feeling uncomfortable being coached by their manager. In some organisations, a traditional approach towards status and positioning within the hierarchy leads to managers adopting a superior attitude. Coaching requires managers to lay aside their position of power over people. One has to work from a more equal relationship to experience the full power of coaching and all of its benefits.

Organisations which have introduced coaching have found that by using coaching contracts the ground rules can be agreed by both parties. This reinforces the coaching concept of equality and win-win scenarios. It is also helpful in the opening conversation to relax both the manager and the direct report. The contract can outline the responsibilities of both the coach and the person being coached, say how sessions will be conducted and set out any other ground rules either party feels are required. The style of the contract will depend upon the culture of the organisation and can take the form of a written document or an informal chat at the first meeting.

Boardroom resistance

It is common to find board members being omitted from the management development process. This may be due to a belief that directors are already at the top of the company, so they must be fully developed! Achievement coaching, which we looked at in Chapter Five is a positive way of developing already successful directors. By giving them experience of the coaching process using an external coach, it is possible to accelerate the change in the board of directors' behaviour towards a coaching style. A frequent cry that we have heard from some personnel professionals is 'If anyone needs coaching in this organisation it is some of our directors.' For any change in management style to be implemented the directors and senior executives must take the concept and not only talk about it but take action upon it. Board members are no different from other managers. They experience similar fears and concerns. Engaging external coaches helps them adapt to the changes that they are facing in the move towards empowered organisations based on flatter structures. Even what might be regarded as hard-nosed managing directors have embarked on development programmes such as the achievement coaching process with great success.

Directors may often believe that coaching is already taking place within their organisation, but this is usually founded on a misconception of coaching. A managing director might say: 'But I already do that. I coach my people. I clarify the issues that need to be addressed, tell them what needs to be done and who is responsible for implementation, and check up to see that they have done it.' This, of course, is a typical command and control approach to coaching. It is mainly task-oriented and it misses out the wider coaching spectrum to realise more potential. The manager does most of the talking, is directive, does not listen and imposes solutions. It may lead to short-term results but it effectively disempowers others. The challenge here is to gain agreement to widen the coaching spectrum and encourage greater behavioural flexibility. Board members and senior executives can be assisted by providing tools for personal development that are completed by the individual and discussed with an independent coach.

Management style

The management style adopted in many organisations is command and control mainly because of the need for task completion. Coaching is in itself a management style insomuch as it is a move away from 'Do what I say' to 'How would you do it?' This may lead to some opposition, as managers may feel threatened and be concerned that they will lose control over what is happening in the business. Clarification of the role of managers is essential. The traditional view of a manager's responsibilities has been:

- organisation
- planning
- delegating
- motivating
- controlling

- training
- leading
- decision-making

With the introduction of quality initiatives and more interaction with employees these responsibilities may now be:

- organisation
- empowering
- coaching
- developing
- leading
- supporting

It could be said that these are the same things under different names, but the behaviour required is totally different.

Managers must understand that they are still required to run the business effectively. The skills required to operate as an empowering manager and assist direct reports through change (as is increasingly happening in modern business) will be developed during the coaching process. The development of direct reports in conjunction with the manager's own development will assist both parties in moving towards the open culture often talked about.

A process to help the direct report is the use of an upward review system, by which the direct report assesses the manager against agreed criteria and this assessment is then fed back during a one-to-one session or at a workshop. In those organisations where this approach has been adopted both manager and direct report have gained a better understanding of each other. It allows the direct report to indicate those areas where the manager could be more supportive, and has been implemented successfully in the banking, manufacturing, retailing, chemical and communication industries.

Further development can follow by implementing the coaching process in the organisation. It is important to remember that to overcome many of the barriers, the involvement of all concerned and training in the system being introduced is essential.

Those organisations where a traditional hierarchical structure still exists are often focused on control and domination. They operate a formal communications process and the employees are not encouraged to contribute to the development of the business other than by following instructions. Such organisations are, however, finding that their structure and culture are, out of necessity, having to change.

When time and energy is spent on developing managers, some change in management style is bound to take place, which will make life better for direct reports. But all too often, a manager returning from a development workshop is filled with enthusiasm for a few days or even weeks, but the effect gradually wears off and direct reports wait for the old style to re-emerge. The result is no change in behaviour or performance. Managers must be enabled to feel comfortable with the change and to practise the new behaviours, but direct reports also require attention if the process is to be long lasting.

Many service industries tend to train front-line staff, who deal directly with customers, but omit to involve management. The development normally takes the form of customer-care training, including some type of interpersonal skills. During such training, comments such as 'It's my manager who should be here, he treats everyone like a child' or 'But that's not what happens in practice' are common. This approach leads to a go-stop situation. The direct report's awareness has been raised but the manager is left behind and continues using old behaviours. Again this reinforces the need for all employees, no matter what their position is, to be actively involved.

The development of both the managers and direct reports is essential if organisations are to survive and prosper into the next decade by optimising the potential of their human resources. This development will provide both with the skills to cope with the many changes with which businesses have to deal. It will encourage an environment in which all employees are in a win-win situation and the organisation's growth is guaranteed. Moving towards this takes time and energy but does not require a lot of money. The employees take responsibility for working out how to achieve business success in their areas for themselves with a little coaching along the way.

Management roles

The key areas to consider when looking at coaching through the eyes of a manager are:

- what is in it for the manager
- the 'no time' factor
- a lack of understanding of the coaching process
- poor interpersonal skills
- a lack of coaching skills
- a fear of the unknown
- a lack of role models
- confusion over the role of the manager
- a lack of evident benefits
- resistance to taking responsibility for staff development

A coaching development programme for all employees is one method of overcoming some of these obstacles. This enables all levels to be included, both those being coached and the coaches themselves. When used with a competency-based management framework it helps to remove some of the fear of the possible intimacy, as it is a more objective structure.

Giving sound business reasons for empowering individuals through developing a coaching approach will maintain the momentum. Focusing on operational requirements will also help overcome the problem of coaching being seen as solely a training initiative.

Most managers feel that they need to be 'sold' or to 'sell' any concept of change. We have already seen the wide range of reasons managers can give for not doing things differently. They may see coaching as just another fad that is going to take even more time away from the real job of managing the people collectively. Being accountable for the actions of a group of people is an aspect of management that can be both appealing and frustrating; by using a coaching process the individual is encouraged to acknowledge that they are responsible and accountable for themselves, freeing some of the time managers spend checking up what their direct reports are doing. It is not taking away any responsibility from the manager but enabling individual direct reports to be more responsible while providing the manager with time for other tasks.

Managers generally do not like to admit that they may have any areas of weakness. As we have already seen, the skills for effective coaching are not new or unachievable, and generally speaking the majority of people possess them. It may be, however, that they are not fully competent in these skills and further development is required. This is where the self-assessment process is beneficial when linked with a process of upward reviewing.

The basic skills of coaching can be developed through workshops and development programmes during the implementation stage. It must be emphasised that all levels within an organisation benefit from this process, and it is crucial for its overall success that all levels are included.

The time factor is another problem. Managers find that much of their time is eaten away by direct reports. Once managers reach the higher stage of competency they find that time does not necessarily have to be allocated specifically for coaching. It is something that takes place on an ongoing basis, both formally and informally. To coach someone through a particular situation you do not need to have a formal process to follow, just some simple questions and the ability to give the other person your attention and listen.

Reward systems

An argument raised in many organisations is that managers are expected to coach direct reports but that this coaching is not assessed in the review or appraisal process. There is no direct correlation between the training and development of direct reports and the achievement of business or individual objectives. In many companies the evaluation of training and development is based only on participants' immediate reactions and not on the longer-term business impact or development that takes place. It is also included in the assessment of training or HR specialists and not the management of the organisation as a whole.

This may be one of the key reasons why managers feel that the training and development of their direct reports has to be carried out by someone else with specialist skills. By introducing a system whereby the development of direct reports is included in managers' agreed objectives and they are assessed on it, managers will become more receptive to the concept. It must become an area where managers can be rewarded for excellence and at the same time be linked to the overall business objectives.

One sales manager in the pharmaceutical industry was convinced of the benefits of putting more time and effort into coaching the individual members of his sales force. After spending more time in the field and coaching them after sales visits he found a significant increase in performance. On joint visits he also ensured that the resulting sales went into their commission structure as a reward. On the appointment of a new sales director he was sacked. The explanation given was that his personal performance targets were too low and he was being outperformed by his own salespeople. His performance measures did not include any reference to his ability to coach and develop his team.

Resistance to transition

Transition can be a stage in our personal development or it can be a major change or challenge in our lives. It is the period during which one style is developing into another, or we are moving from one set of circumstances to another. A common barrier to effective coaching is a lack of understanding of the resistance individuals feel to the process.

When you begin to coach people you will notice different approaches to resisting the changes that are taking place. This is not only concerned with the resistance to the concept itself but also resistance that the individual may feel during the coaching process. Understanding the stages of transition will help you to cope with your own resistance and that of your direct reports. It will also enable you to identify some of the tell-tale signs at each stage and assist in moving people forward.

No matter what the subject or situation, there can be a natural resistance to change. It may be cultural, when the values of the organisation are affected, seen when external consultants are used; social, when changes threaten to affect relationships, seen when the norms are challenged; organisational, when change interferes with status or the formal status quo; or psychological,

Figure 6.1
The transition curve

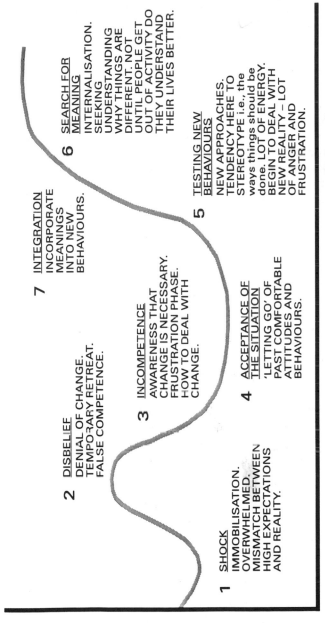

COMPETENCE

TIME

Beginning of
Transition

1 SHOCK
IMMOBILISATION.
OVERWHELMED.
MISMATCH BETWEEN
HIGH EXPECTATIONS
AND REALITY.

2 DISBELIEF
DENIAL OF CHANGE.
TEMPORARY RETREAT.
FALSE COMPETENCE.

3 INCOMPETENCE
AWARENESS THAT
CHANGE IS NECESSARY.
FRUSTRATION PHASE.
HOW TO DEAL WITH
CHANGE.

**4 ACCEPTANCE OF
THE SITUATION**
'LETTING GO' OF
PAST COMFORTABLE
ATTITUDES AND
BEHAVIOURS.

**5 TESTING NEW
BEHAVIOURS**
NEW APPROACHES.
TENDENCY HERE TO
STEREOTYPE i.e., the
ways things should be
done. LOT OF ENERGY.
BEGIN TO DEAL WITH
NEW REALITY – LOT
OF ANGER AND
FRUSTRATION.

**6 SEARCH FOR
MEANING**
INTERNALISATION.
SEEKING
UNDERSTANDING
WHY THINGS ARE
DIFFERENT. NOT
UNTIL PEOPLE GET
OUT OF ACTIVITY DO
THEY UNDERSTAND
THEIR LIVES BETTER.

7 INTEGRATION
INCORPORATE
MEANINGS
INTO NEW
BEHAVIOURS.

when an individual sees it as not being beneficial. For any of these the resistance is seen through behaviour.

Understanding the transition process through change and the typical behaviour displayed helps in the management both of self and of others. Figure 6.1 shows the seven stages of people's reaction to change.

For each of these stages there are common behaviours and statements to look for.

1. **Shock**. Normally this manifests itself as total immobilisation. The first time news of change is given the statement 'I need time to take this in' is often heard. Allow the individual to process the information, stay quiet and watch. When there has been a change in job roles other typical comments include 'Did I really apply for this job?' and 'This is not the job I expected.'

2. **Disbelief**. This is when individuals use behaviours which were appropriate once but are inappropriate in the new situation. This can be dysfunctional if it goes on too long. The tendency to behave as if nothing has changed and try to ignore what is happening can be seen whenever change takes place. Support from others is required if people are going to move on to the next stage. At this point coaching is an ideal tool for assisting them through the process.

   The typical statements used include: 'The last time I did this I . . .'; 'This is very similar to . . .'; and 'I will do the same as . . . They will forget in time.'

3. **Incompetence**. This is when there is a feeling of depression and flatness. An ability to cope with the new situation leads to confusion and frustration, often seen in angry and reactive behaviour. It is a necessary stage if people are to come to terms with the change. Support is required to enable them to cope.

   Typical statements include: 'I'm not sure what to do'; 'What's going on?'; and 'I can't get to grips with this.'

4. **Acceptance of the situation**. For the first time past behaviours and views are disregarded. Future opportunities are now considered and there is a general feeling of relief. The behaviour becomes much more positive and the level of competence begins to rise.

Statements include 'I know where I was going wrong, I'm going to try . . .'; and 'I understand what is different and I can now do . . .'

5. **Testing new behaviours**. This is a time when a lot of activity takes place and there can be displays of anger and frustration when things are not going as expected. Assistance during this period is essential and if there is a time when poor management can cause long-term damage it is likely to be at this stage. It is inevitable that mistakes will be made, and rather than holding these against the person they should be encouraged to continue in the process.

Statements used at this stage include: 'Let's try another way'; 'We need to do it like this . . .'; and 'It's not worked like that, let's look for an alternative.'

6. **Searching for meaning**. This is a period of reflection on the processes which have taken place and an attempt to understand the emotions experienced. Often it is at this stage that people begin to share their feelings and views about the period of change.

7. **Integration**. The transition is over. We now see stability in the conditions surrounding the change event. People have learned or adopted new behaviours and display signs of optimum competence in the situation.

Typical statements include: 'I'm glad that's over, but I've learnt a lot'; and 'I understand what it's about and I feel like a new person.'

It is important to remember that some people may get stuck at various stages. They may never move on from disbelief or may give up in a state of depression. In the same way there are those who can move through the transition very quickly but will none the less experience all the stages. For people to cope fully with this process, support and encouragement is required and coaching provides this in a way that is not threatening to the individual.

Appraisal and review systems

The fact that organisations have an appraisal system does not mean that the employees see it as a rewarding or beneficial process. In the task-oriented organisation there are many objections to carrying out an appraisal, many of which are similar to the objections to coaching:

- lack of time
- poor planning
- a concern that appraisals are too subjective
- a feeling that they are a waste of time
- fear

The purpose of the appraisal can be to improve current performance, provide feedback, increase motivation, identify training needs, identify potential, let individuals know what is expected of them, focus on career development, award salary increases, solve job problems (normally problems in the appraisee's job as seen by the appraiser), set job performance objectives and serve as a reward or punishment in itself. The coaching process is often seen by direct reports as a way for managers to direct and implement an alternative form of appraisal.

Many organisations are benefiting from using coaching to implement an upward appraisal system. It enables managers to gain a clear understanding of their direct reports' needs. Programmes using this approach have been very successful in the retailing, chemical, banking and other industries. It is sometimes met with some trepidation from managers but in those companies where it has been fully introduced all aspects of the company have developed. This form of appraisal is based upon a coaching style where the direct report discusses areas of performance where they would benefit from a different approach by the manager, or where support is required. It is important to emphasise that this approach will bring about a culture change from a controlling, dominating style to an empowered, facilitative style.

It must be remembered that this process will initially need a lot of time but the long-term results will be good. Ask any organisation what the main internal problem is which it has to overcome, and you will usually be told that it is improving communication within the company. This is an area we would all like to think we are good at, but it is also one of the main areas managers see as being a problem. Through the introduction of effective coaching systems many organisations have found that communication improves, as well as personal satisfaction and time planning.

Good coaches are always looking for ways to improve and learn faster and they are also receptive to coaching themselves. Poor coaches are dogmatic, inflexible, self-righteous and resistant to coaching themselves. One way to respond to the latter is to ask them questions. Get them to think about what they are doing and its implications while at the same time suggesting small steps for improvement. Go with the open door though. If you hit a brick wall, work on other more receptive areas. There are unfortunately plenty of command and control managers who are actually feared by their staff, and the challenge is to coach them into adopting a coaching style of management.

A quick guide to coaching

Barriers to coaching

- organisational hierarchies creating power over people
- board-level behaviours and lack of role models
- management style
- management responsibilities not seen to include staff development
- lack of coaching skills
- reward systems
- resistance to transition
- appraisal and review systems

The challenge to any organisation is what it does to overcome these and other obstacles to enable it to grow.

7

The Role of the Development Professional

Introduction

The ever-changing environment of work has, over the past ten years, left organisations in a constant state of flux. Smaller personnel and training functions are now becoming the norm. Gone are the days when armies of HR professionals were attached to organisations and were often seen as an additional cost, and as having no perceived visible impact upon the business. In fact during the recessional 1980s and 1990s the personnel and training functions were among the first to be hit with cutbacks in staffing levels.

Alongside these trends, the management gurus were proffering a variety of solutions on how to reorganise company structures and develop quality systems and procedures. They put forward ideas on how to encourage employee empowerment, improve customer service, re-engineering and many more. Little wonder that managers found themselves in a constant state of turmoil, as they did not know what to expect next.

It is no surprise that many of these methods involved some participation from training and development specialists. Most required clear developmental processes inside the organisation, and these were often serviced by external consultants who were perceived as having the expertise in particular fields such as team development, communication systems or quality initiatives. It became paramount for those organisations who wished to survive the troubled times to keep constantly ahead of their competitors.

Now more than ever, successful companies are trying new approaches in their attempt to stay at the top. With the constant momentum to meet ever-changing market requirements, businesses have adopted a fast and bullish approach towards maintaining status in highly competitive markets. There is little or no room for those companies which follow trends today. If it is going to stay in business, the company must be a trend-*setter*! People are being asked to overcome entrenched beliefs and attitudes towards work and are expected to make a greater contribution to the running of the business. However they are not often given any help in dealing with the pace of change and the demands made upon them.

Inevitably organisations have looked to internal training and development consultants to help address some of these issues. Managers are now required to train and develop their staff, maintain appropriate records for staff development (a key aspect of IIP) and empower their staff. In some instances they have to recruit staff and at the same time complete their own ever-increasing workload. HR and training professionals are therefore key change agents within organisations. Their role is to provide managers with the necessary tools to complete these demanding tasks successfully. Now more than ever the personnel/HR/development professional also needs to be fully conversant with all the financial aspects of their business, to demonstrate that they are commercially aware and have good business acumen.

We are now looking at how the development professional can, through the introduction of coaching, fully assist managers to meet the challenges of these demanding times head on.

Changing cultures

As we have said, development professionals can have a major impact on culture change. The following process is one that we have successfully adopted.

1. **Establish what the core business of the company is**. This allows the senior team to refocus on the true element of their business. In many instances companies forget what that core element is and find themselves moving off track in many directions, without having a significant impact in any. As a highly successful insurance manager in a company that had undergone a merger of two divisions once said, 'I understand insurance, and I'm not prepared for the addition of selling holidays to distract me from that.'
2. **Discover what the current state of the culture is**. The most

effective way to gain this information is to ask. Senior managers may well tell you what they believe the culture is, but this may be far from the reality.

3. **Evaluate how coaching would enhance the current culture or business performance**. What would the pay-offs be for the business?

4. **If a culture change is desired, establish where does the organisation want to be**. What does it want to be different in the new regime? What, therefore, does it need to do in order to move towards this new culture?

5. **Work out who will be doing what, where and when**. How will the changes be communicated to all the employees and their agreement and commitment be gained? How will the organisation know when they have got there? What will be happening? What changes will be evident following any change initiative?

6. **Decide what is the best and the worst that could happen if the initiative is carried out.** What is the best and the worst that would happen if nothing is changed? This helps you decide the benefits and pay-offs.

During the early stages of this process it is essential that senior managers and directors are assisted in dealing with all aspects of the questions asked. This is crucial if the message is going to be successfully passed down the company hierarchy. It will also help if all opinions are objectively assembled and the correct data obtained. The development professional can offer assistance with this by facilitating meetings and coaching senior managers through the process.

In many companies development professionals have been used to introduce the message to employees via team-building programmes and communication systems development. They have facilitated standards working parties and the introduction of operational standards training manuals. They have been responsible for heightening employees' customer awareness and many more such initiatives supporting the desired changes.

The skills of an effective coach are essential for development and HR professionals when bringing about changes in company culture. The commitment of the boardroom to change and agreement on what has to happen to bring about the change can only be gained through effective coaching. The basic principle of agreeing that something needs to be done and then allowing the individual to come up with the best solution for them is exactly the same.

The advantage of an internal consultant is that they will stay on with the company to see the process through. Many external consultants do the job without being totally familiar with the company politics, and then leave to tackle another organisation. It is only rare consultancies which develop a long-term relationship with the client and stay on to ensure complete success, even when the so-called training has finished. Whenever consultants are used to assist with a change process or development initiative it is important that the values are clearly defined and any change is framed in such a way as to enhance those values.

As with the coaching process, consultants must follow the languaging patterns of the company. Every organisation has its own terminology, even those from the same industry, and the HR specialist must ensure that the consultants talk the same language, otherwise people will be disbelieving.

Integration with business strategy

For many years the evaluation of training and development has been linked to the objectives of the organisation. With such initiatives as Investors in People even more emphasis is placed on this approach. This means that all training and development must have clear business measures that are understood by the manager and the direct report. There must be evidence that the individual undergoing development has a commitment to some type of personal action plan and that this is reviewed at regular intervals by their manager.

With the introduction of coaching this review process can become an everyday occurrence. Managers become particularly interested in the process when they are talking about improvements in business results. This is not to be mistaken with the traditional review or appraisal systems where yearly objectives are discussed. Any evaluation process needs to be precise and simple, especially if it is intended to be used by the manager and direct report. The training professional must ensure that any documentation used is business-linked and can allow for a continual development process to take place.

The effect of coaching on an organisation can be seen in core elements, namely:

- philosophies values and culture – the accepted behaviours
- practices – systems and procedures
- people
- products – whatever the outputs are, whether service or items
- profits

The philosophies of the organisation will have a direct effect upon what practices are adopted and installed. In the same way these practices are what the people see and use. Ask any employee in your company to name three values, describe the culture or give the philosophies of the organisation and they will probably have some difficulty in providing you with an answer. This is mainly because the vast majority of employees do not have anything tangible to hook into. However if there is something drastically wrong with the culture or values they will pick it up. The practices, systems or procedures used in the company can more readily be recognised, and employees automatically know what you are looking for.

The people, through the practices, will have a direct impact upon the product your company is involved with, whether a tangible product or a service. The final area all companies are concerned with, of course, the ultimate aim, is profit. By using coaching throughout the company all areas can be developed and improved. This will become a continual cycle of improvement and growth, just what the management gurus say is required to stay ahead of the competition.

But how do you persuade people of the benefits for the company of a coaching approach? A training manager in a division of a large organisation once said: 'How do I get the senior team on board? How can I put forward the case for change in such a way that they are committed to its implementation? They are tough-minded business people who see training as being something that is done to employees in order to get them to obtain maximum sales and therefore profits. I just don't seem to be able to win them over!'

This is a common enough situation, where you have a group of task-driven managers, out for profit at all costs, who do not see the value of training or development if it is not task- or skills-driven. They are not interested in 'airy fairy' ideas, only in profit. Here are some tips for dealing with such people: *selling" coaching in aco.*

- Talk to them in their language; avoid developmental jargon.
- Ask them how they think a solution for improvement can be found. Do they have any ideas? Use those valuable coaching skills!
- Offer them a solution that matches their views.
- Close with questions which will gain their agreement to your solution.
- Make sure you include them at all stages of the proposal as well as the implementation.
- Highlight what might happen if they do nothing, both in terms of the best and worst possibilities.
- Highlight what might happen if they go ahead with the proposal, again in terms of the worst and best possible outcomes.

In this way the senior managers will feel that they have made a major contribution to the solution.

A training manager who had successfully introduced a management development programme into an organisation said, 'I really don't know what I've said or done, but the whole operations team are so eager to become involved it is almost frightening. They have to be held back at times. There is so much enthusiasm around the place it's just like a dream!' Upon investigation it became clear that the keys to this success included:

- looking at the real needs of the business, both actual and as perceived by senior management
- matching training to all these needs
- relating the training to the business
- gaining commitment from the very top down
- involving the business operations at all stages of the process, including the delivery of some of the programmes
- giving support to those delivering training as well as those making the business work.

Trainers as coaches/facilitators

Trainers are used to providing delegates with a programme that will be followed, although there is usually some discussion at the start of a training session about the objectives of the course and how the trainer will achieve them. In theory there is absolutely nothing wrong with this approach; it provides a clear outline of what the purpose of the course is. Generally, however, the trainer has a pre-set programme which they will follow whether or not it is needed. This is no longer enough. The flexibility now expected from employees extends to in-house trainers as well.

A medium-sized manufacturing company bought a development programme for potential senior managers to attend from a well known and respected external management business school. The opening session started in true training fashion with the trainer outlining the objectives and the content of each module. When he came to service quality one of the participants asked 'Who are *your* customers then? The trainer said that they, the delegates, were. 'Why haven't you asked us what we want then? asked the participant. This led to a radical rethink of the course agenda and instead of participants having to complete every module, whether they needed them or not, a menu of modules was offered. The trainer was so upset by this whole process that a replacement was found.

So what does this tell trainers?

- Check any external training consultants, since they must fit into the culture of your company.
- Develop a 'tool-box' of materials and knowledge that will enable you to be flexible.
- Remember that if a coaching approach is being used the trainer also needs to adopt the same style. This means much more input from the participants and less input from you.
- 'Walk the talk'! Show by example.

If an organisation is adopting coaching, it follows that the trainer/developer must be prepared to change their style also. This involves adopting a facilitative style, being prepared to go with the flow and rather than telling people, guiding them through to reach conclusions. This sounds easy, but standing in front of or sitting with a group of senior managers can be frightening.

The changing role of trainers is to become the coach for the coaches. This involves coaching managers, direct reports, your boss and those external organisations that have contact with your company. It is essential that you coach them, as this is not an easy approach with overnight success; you have to be prepared for some opposition.

Applications within the HR function

Competency development

Throughout the last decade the use of job competencies has become an integral part of employee assessment, development and selection. These competencies relate to core areas of performance for any level of employee in an organisation and reflect its culture and values. They are described in behavioural terms to show organisation's expectations of its employees.

Using coaching as a management style can be extremely effective in encouraging employees to take responsibility and accountability for their own development. It is an objective assessment of the individual's behaviours against those the company expects. Where the individual is below the expected norm coaching can help them to find their own solutions for improvement.

When looking at succession planning within any organisation the use of a competency framework will obviously be a valuable tool. It provides objective evidence of each member of the team or management within the company and highlights areas to be developed to meet the future needs of the business. Using coaching on a regular basis also provides managers with a greater insight into the capabilities of their direct reports when considering promotions and additional responsibilities, and can encourage individuals to realise their full potential. After someone has completed some major task one will often hear them say, 'I never realised I could do it.' If you use coaching alongside competencies, people practise improvements before there is any time pressure, and you can avoid 'sink or swim' situations.

Assessment centres

Assessment centres are being used for both external and internal people with increased frequency. For job selection it is an ideal way of getting the right person for the role. HR functions can increase the success of such events, especially for internal people, by using coaching when giving feedback to delegates, rather than just telling them they are above or below standard and leaving them to deal with it on their own. By coaching the individual you can not only get them to identify their own successes or failures but they also own the solutions.

It is not surprising that people need support in coming to terms with success as well as failure. Removing limiting beliefs can take time. Simply telling someone they are successful is not sufficient; they will want to see evidence as well. Coach them to find their own evidence.

Induction programmes

The induction of new employees generally takes place to some degree or other in most companies. Part of the process includes reviewing what the new employee has done and learned. By using coaching at this stage the review is not so formal and it will enable the employee to draw up their own action plan for further development. Coaching can take place at any time or place and will develop better working relationships between the manager and new recruit. This is also important in graduate recruitment to overcome the high drop-out rate.

Appraisals and annual reviews

The success of any appraisal or review system depends on the skills of those carrying out the appraisal. As we have already seen, managers are not always keen to implement them. It is often seen as a time to give the direct report a long list of objectives and things that are not working or must be corrected. Management by objectives, however, is no longer seen as the most efficient way of achieving results.

The appraisal must be a two-way process, and introducing both upward and downward coaching and reviews requires both parties to have an input into the discussion. We do not propose to spend time in this book looking at how to improve managers' appraisal skills, but we are keen to link the appraisal or review with coaching and personal development plans, for in this way companies are better equipped to develop a learning style organisation.

Redundancy

During the past two decades redundancy has become almost commonplace and it is no longer seen as an opportunity to remove people. It has become the trend in downsizing companies in order to make savings and to re-engineer processes. This has opened the door for specialist career counselling, redundancy counselling and outplacement all of which, if carried out by external consultants, will be expensive.

Explaining that it is the job and not the individual that is no longer required may not help the person concerned to come to terms with the sudden change. Moving people from a state of shock to acceptance and thinking about the future needs to be done carefully. Some consultants and HR specialists get into difficulties when discussing future opportunities too quickly in the change process. If someone is in denial, no matter how much you ask them to think about the next step or what opportunities there are available to them, you will still meet a blank wall.

By developing coaching skills it is possible to match, model and pace the individual's behaviour, gradually moving them towards a positive resource state. It is at this point that future-paced coaching questions can be used to develop a clear action plan and commitment to the future possibilities. The general view held by many outplacement consultants is that to assist anyone through redundancy you must have experienced it for yourself. There is some validity in this but with coaching you do not have to know from experience in order to give positive help.

Personal development plans

Personal development plans (PDPs) have in recent years developed from one-page attachments to appraisal forms to booklets in their own right. The concept of learning organisations has encouraged many organisations to design and implement a customised PDP. Managers have been encouraged to take responsibility for their own development and to promote learning as an everyday occurrence.

In general terms learning organisations take every opportunity to learn both from experience and at individual, group and corporate level, inducing a climate where learning from each other is fostered and actively supported, leading to a facilitative style of management and a continuous development cycle. These organisations generally see learning as an integral part of the company growth and look to evolve through promoting questions, stimulating two-way communications, fostering the idea that experimentation and exploration are permitted and removing any barriers and blockages to learning both in the individual and in the environment. The personal development planner has an influential and powerful influence on how successful any company is in becoming a 'learning organisation'. The success of the PDP depends to a large extent on the coaching skills of management within the company as well as on how effectively the internal HR specialist has introduced the process throughout the company.

What is included in the plan very much depends upon the culture of each individual company but a minimum outline for content would include a record of:

- competence assessment and action plan for developing any of the competencies
- learning record log for both formal, off-the-job, and informal learning activities
- other learning activities which otherwise might have been missed by the individual

For each section the employee will be encouraged to record how the new learning will be used in the work situation and what benefits, in business and personal terms, will be achieved.

More comprehensive plans may include an individual's career to date, action planning and a personal journal and learning diary, which will cover areas such as:

- a career to date interview where the coach asks a series of questions to find out the factors that guided and constrained the individual's career, such as education, jobs taken and reasons for changing jobs, what has been enjoyed or not enjoyed to date in the career concerned
- a CV document outlining any significant gaps in terms of achievement both in and outside work and educational/development achievements
- some form of self-assessment and awareness exercises – these normally make use of a psychometric diagnostic and may also include feedback from others that helps the employee to gain a clearer picture of themselves
- goal-setting – looking at what the individual wants out of their career, personal development and personal life, stating what they must do in order to achieve the desired goals
- action planning for each goal, outlining the success criteria, the benefits, possible hurdles to overcome, programme of development activities and an outline of the review progress to be followed

The PDP is just that; personal and to be kept by the individual. It is not to be used to catch people out but to promote growth in the company.

However, PDPs are doomed to failure unless the employees can see the benefit to themselves. All too often they are introduced as a company benefit and not an all-round benefit. It is also important that the documents, no matter how small or large, must be simple to understand and complete.

The language of the PDP needs to take a coaching style if it is going to generate innovation and commitment by the user. There are organisations which have introduced a PDP and found it to be totally ineffective. One reason for this is that managers were introduced to a mammoth document, looking at aspects alien to both the culture and the manager. They expected the manager to take the process on board when they may not even have been fully implementing the appraisal system. It is essential that the first PDP be relevant to the manager, not too adrift from the current culture, relevant to the industry norms and simple to use. All of these may seem common sense, but when you become involved it is all too easy to design another personnel fad. Once introduced the original can be developed to reflect how the organisation develops in this area.

Summary

The constantly changing face of industry, commerce and the public sector means that for HR functions to keep ahead of trends they must be prepared to change their own behaviours and roles. At the strategic level the HR function can now have a positive impact on the continued success of the company.

Coaching the trainers so that they can deliver facilitative development programmes is crucial. The understanding of behavioural science has become a prerequisite for any training and development specialist, especially when many organisational or cultural initiatives demand their support and involvement.

Coaching fits into any of the routine personnel functions and systems. It will assist in bringing about positive culture change and will enhance the potential of the workforce. Organisations embarking upon processes of continuous improvement will find that by using coaching as a method for developing individual accountability and responsibility, the process of producing quality goods and services is enhanced dramatically.

Case Studies

Introduction

As coaching becomes more commonplace in business practice there is an accumulating body of evidence of the success that results from adopting a coaching style. Different approaches to coaching have been around for many years, from the instructing style to the more developmental and empowering approach advocated by this book. Many people have experienced working for a manager who adopted a coaching approach and as a result they gave more in terms of energy and effort through greater commitment and higher productivity. Conversely, more people have experienced the old but familiar command and control style that may get short-term results but can lead to frustrated people feeling disempowered and therefore not giving of their best.

Undoubtedly many individuals within organisations have already found coaching working for them despite the overall approach of most company cultures which reinforces a command and control style of management. It is only in recent years that company-wide commitments have been made to developing coaching capability for competitive advantage. At Rover Group, line managers have shifted from being 'cops' to 'coaches' with the aim of developing staff to make the most of their skills and deal effectively with the massive changes facing the motor vehicle manufacturing industry. At Rothmans, coaching is also one of the many skills line managers must have to be good leaders, and it is acknowledged that the learning culture at the company, of which coaching is a vital part, has helped cut absenteeism and job turnover levels. Motorola are committed to developing coaching capability in order to stay ahead of the competition by using their knowledge-workers to best effect.

Public-sector bodies are also turning to coaching as a key element in helping managers optimise the skills and talents of their staff. Peter Wormald, Registrar General of the Office of

Population Censuses & Surveys sees the introduction of coaching throughout the department as a tool for staff development. It is this kind of support from the top of more and more organisations which is leading to the build-up of momentum in creating higher levels of coaching competence.

The drive to reduce lead times down the supply chain has led to a move away from the adversarial, 'put the screws on the supplier' approach. Now more and more successful companies are engaged in developing better relationships with their suppliers by using a coaching approach to gain a better understanding of each other's requirements.

Brooke Bond Foods Ltd

The main Brooke Bond Food tea factory, home of PG Tips, is located on the Trafford Park Industrial Estate in Manchester. Major investment was made in the site to upgrade its manufacturing capability and concentrate all tea-packing on one site. Supermarket and wholesale customers were demanding shorter delivery lead times and a greater degree of personalised service.

Against a history of being a 'problem site' because of difficulties in meeting production requirements first time, a new management team was assembled to upgrade the operations of the factory and manage substantial changes in improving the manufacturing facility and developing improved working practices. The factory management team was made up of highly competent, well-qualified professionals intent on achieving the task of factory improvements.

A coaching project was initiated by the Factory Manager, Dr Martin Powell, to accelerate the process of teamworking throughout the site. There were still some adversarial relationships amongst the management team, which also created some conflict amongst assistant managers and operatives. The main focus of the coaching project was to improve teamworking amongst members of the management team. Success criteria were set to measure the effectiveness of using a coaching process rather than conventional team-building training courses.

An agreement to undertake a process to improve teamworking was put by the Factory Manager to the management team for approval. He still remembers the audible sigh of relief that went around the meeting as they acknowledged the need to do something. He later recalled the effectiveness of the approach by saying, 'When people recognise the issue of teamworking, do something about it. If they do not recognise it as an issue, don't.'

One-to-one coaching meetings were held, using a professional coach, to identify the individual perceptions of how the team worked together and how they would like to work together. This was followed by an 'awayday' to consolidate plans for the year ahead and work on issues relating to teamworking. The coaching project continued over the next 18 months with a series of individual coaching meetings and team 'awaydays'. The one-to-one meetings were initially based around a structured, survey approach which then developed into more freewheeling coaching conversations.

At the same time an in-house project was already under way to achieve reductions in line changeover times by adopting a coaching approach involving production operators. Some lines took in excess of 14 hours to change over, leading to delays in meeting production targets. One of the supervisors, Jack Young, gained the commitment of the technical operators to aim for significant improvements. By empowering the team through using his natural, people-oriented, coaching style, Jack was able to achieve significant improvements leading to a reduction in changeover times to under 2 hours. The sense of pride and enthusiasm for their jobs on the shop floor was infectious. 'We have become more confident and self-aware,' said one of the team, Gary Burnett. 'We love solving problems; all decision-making is done within the group and as a result the attitude is right within the team.'

The management team achieved their site objectives by sharing team responsibilities and objectives. There was improved communication and a sense of belonging with increased confidence in being able to focus on individual actions with support from the rest of the team. The factory was acknowledged as having improved though increased recognition of the effectiveness of operations on site and gained considerable publicity in the company newsletter. This led to an article in the Engineering Council's newsletter on 'Continuing Professional Development' which is now used as case study material by the Open University.

A BBC video on coaching, *Coaching for Results* also features the line improvement team in action.

Office of Population Censuses & Surveys

The Office of Population Censuses & Surveys (OPCS) is the government department that produces demographic, social and medical information and analysis so that the number and condition of the population can be monitored, and changes over time identified. It also administers the marriage laws and the registration of births, marriages and deaths. Against a background of increasing pressure to limit public expenditure, it has embarked upon a long-term strategy to equip staff to adapt their products and services to meet the fast-changing needs of their customers.

Developing the coaching capabilities of managerial grades was part of the strategy to accelerate the process of change by using coaching to support staff development. It was decided to create a critical mass of staff committed to coaching in order to raise confidence in the process at an early stage.

A series of coaching skills workshops was run across all the senior grades using outside coaching consultants. Close liaison and monitoring of the project was undertaken by the Training and Development Unit, which also took the project on board for eventual implementation by in-house trainers throughout all the managerial grades.

The first coaching workshop was run for heads of department and then with their approval was cascaded down over a period of two years throughout the organisation. The coaching workshops were highly participative and experiential by nature, dealing with a series of coaching models applied to real-life current situations. By engaging in practical coaching exercises which could be related to the workplace there was a high transference of skills and an increase in competence. There was a commitment to reinforce the process by organised self-help learning groups and building coaching sessions into forward job planning.

A series of surveys conducted after participants had been through the workshops indicated some early short-term gains which served as evidence of the successful implementation of coaching plans. Some of the comments that came out of the follow-up surveys were:

- Coaching techniques have helped me to help people find their own solutions to problems.
- Three individuals tackled and completed tasks successfully which they would previously not have done well, largely through fear and lack of support.
- We have just about got my section and myself out of the panic zone. This now means that I can have structured meetings which focus on the matters in hand and get a positive result at the end of it.
- I can delegate a complete task from start to finish to a member of my team who previously lacked confidence in her ability to manage the task. By using both the models and techniques I felt that coaching helped her complete the task successfully.
- I tried to implement coaching but not everyone responds positively, so I need to find other ways.
- With a person who disliked intensely the new job he had been put into because it was all new to him and he was no longer the acknowledged expert, we decided that it was better for him to look at the growing list of things he could do in his new job rather than depress himself by focusing on the list of things he could not yet do.

The coaching project was initiated just before a new performance review system was introduced across the department. Using coaching techniques as part of the performance reviews helped to implement the new system and reinforce the process. As with all interventions of this nature there was some initial resistance to the coaching workshops. Some participants were reluctant to attend and only came because of a 'three-line whip' and the public commitment to the programme from the top of the organisation. Some felt that they were already coaching – even if their staff did not.

Reinforcement of the coaching process continued with self-help groups set up by participants to share ideas and examples of successful implementation. Further in-house trainer-led workshops and a number of mini-workshops were conducted by managers with their staff to develop coaching capability.

Motorola

Motorola is a market leader in the worldwide telecommunications industry. Its business in the United Kingdom has expanded rapidly in the last few years. The company training plan includes the competencies that each employee needs in a year's time in order to meet the needs of each division's strategy. Technology training is based on a five-year forward view of the company's real needs. Sales per employee have doubled during the past five years and profits increased by almost 50 per cent.

The Cellular Subscriber Division in the UK was introduced to a coaching process as part of the General Manager's vision of growing the business. The commitment was made by the top team to develop coaching as part of the culture. It was encouraged throughout the organisation, between peers, managers and staff, individuals and their bosses.

Workshops were run for managers so that they could be seen as the leaders and role models for coaching. The managers in turn committed themselves to run workshops for their teams to cascade the process which was also reinforced with the introduction of PDPs. People were encouraged to find their own coaches, which meant that some managers were more in demand than others, according to their competence as coaches and personal preference.

Being able to help managers realise the potential of the workforce was one of the main benefits. Jo Hughes, Motorola's Training Manager, advises other companies considering the introduction of a coaching culture to focus on business benefits. 'It is dangerous to view coaching solely as a training initiative,' she says. 'For it to be successful it has got to be something that is taken on as a business issue which training can then support. As an isolated training initiative it will quickly lose its appeal.'

In her division, virtually the entire top team changed over three years. The resulting lack of stability prevented them from reinforcing the commitment from the top to a coaching culture. It was difficult to maintain consistency with the aims that were originally set. Although there are still plenty of signs of the original coaching programme, they are not so strong. It needed integrating into all parts of 'the way we do business' on a daily basis to gradually change the culture of the organisation over at least a five year period. In a task-oriented business it is very easy to get drawn into achieving the tasks. 'Unless there is some clear goal of objectives for line managers in the area of people development it is very difficult to keep it at the forefront,' concludes Jo Hughes.

Kalamazoo System Print

Peter White, Managing Director of Kalamazoo System Print (KSP), is an advocate of the achievement coaching process. 'In the competitive business of print, business forms and paper systems we have to maintain the edge by leading the market. Achievement coaching helps bring out the best in us.'

KSP, based in Birmingham, has undergone a transformation in the 18 months since Peter White joined them. The company, which was making substantial losses, is now producing considerable profits. This is a performance turnaround worth millions of pounds, a remarkable achievement which has been made possible in part by focusing the resources of the organisation and using a coaching approach to lever up the business.

Tough decisions had to be made and risks taken in order to reach demanding goals. KSP has been around for 100 years and is very resistant to change. 'We have invested in technology and streamlined processes,' said White. 'We have also invested in people to build this business up again.' His commitment to coaching goes back to his days as a participant on a Leadership Trust programme. After successfully completing the programme he was asked to join the team of industry-based tutors. Since then he has applied his leadership and coaching skills to advantage as a managing director of a number of different organisations. 'Coaching is a skill which managers need to learn. It is essential that you get in touch with your personal power and perform at the highest level,' he said. 'Coaching is helping Kalamazoo System Print grow and adapt to change faster than ever before.'

Gripple

Gripple Ltd is a small, innovative manufacturing company with world-class ambitions. Entrepreneurially driven by Hugh Facey, the Managing Director, it has grown significantly in the last five years with a unique product and system for joining and tensioning fencing and trellising.

Committed to an informal management structure where individuals accept responsibilities and challenges and work in teams to achieve success, Gripple has developed a coaching culture. The achievement coaching process has been applied to develop a flatter structure and encourage open and honest communication. Hugh Facey made a conscious decision to adopt a coaching approach in order to create an empowering environment. Supported by the use of an external coach, members of the management team have used coaching techniques with customers, suppliers, staff and each other to good effect.

Delivery times have been reduced and there are faster response times in order processing. Monthly goals and targets are to the forefront with good liaison between production and sales. 'Coaching is not a magic panacea,' says Facey, 'but by concentrating on bringing out the best in people it empowers them to realise their potential for their own benefit and that of the business.' Using the coaching process in the manufacturing side of the business has led to greater productivity with fewer mistakes and fewer quality problems. It has helped to develop the role of team members and make the transition from a controlling approach to a coaching style. John Woodhead, Production Foreman, says, 'I trust people to get on and do the job without interference from me. Coaching them enables me to pass on my knowledge and experience. I make suggestions for improvement but they think it through themselves. As a result my phone bill at home has gone down dramatically with fewer calls from the factory with problems that they now feel able to solve themselves.'

Rover Group

Rover was one of the first companies to uses the phrase 'cops to coaches' when describing the management style they were intent on developing throughout the group.

Committed to becoming internationally renowned for extraordinary customer satisfaction they embarked on a major process of change. Rover believes that people who are constantly learning are people who are more receptive to change. To help it achive its ambitious aims it launched Rover Learning Business (RLB) in 1990, committed to providing a continuous learning environment. One of its core objectives was to unlock and recognise employee talents and to make better use of them. Doug Dickson, the Director of Vehicle Assembly at the Longbridge plant and now Managing Director of RLB, saw that, in their new roles, line managers needed to lead within a changed management culture. It was he who coined the phrase 'cops to coaches' to describe the change. The role of line managers now is to support employees and help them make the most of their skills in a climate of total quality.

The role of the training professionals in RLB and the Business Unit Learning and Development Departments, is to supply a service to their internal customers which includes a range of learning and development activities. Trainers now working as change agents supporting the change process have no formal authority over the multi-functional teams with which they work. They have had to develop a coaching approach to get the best out of others and reach agreed objectives. Although Rover does not label people as coaches, they promote and support a coaching style for project leaders and within the line management roles. The way managers go about leading is to create the climate for others to make things happen.

RLB provides resources in different ways to meet operational requirements. Their Coaching for Excellence programme provides tools and materials for line managers to implement their own coaching process. The initial programme developed for leaders in strategic positions at the centre of Rover Group is now led by a small team of participants from that first programme. The new participants are people from their departments. It has proved very powerful to integrate 'off the job' training with 'on the job' applications to real work issues. Although the focus is primarily on raising performance and the development of skills and knowledge, the move is towards encouraging creativity and behavioural change.

As Rover move closer towards becoming a learning organisation, the coaching approach has enabled them to realise more of their employees' potential. The link to business needs in their change management process has seen significant improvements in products and an enhanced image in the marketplace.

National & Provincial Building Society

The National & Provincial Building Society (N&P), based in Bradford, is committed to a process-based approach to management. Under the direction of David O'Brien, the Chief Executive, the focus is on meeting the needs of customers by designing quality into the organisation. One of the results has been that N&P was amongst the first financial institutions to encourage customers to take advantage of higher interest rates on their savings accounts. Through their Bee Guided Initiative (a pun on the society's logo of a bee), they reviewed individual accounts with customers. This approach of guiding and advising, reflected in their management philosophy, led to over a million new and existing customers moving to a better account for their needs.

The vision of the society is to create a management style of advising, guiding and coaching, rather than command and control. David O'Brien uses a footballing analogy to get across the messsage of team-play. N&P people play together in teams with the Team Leader as coach. All players have the same set of competencies but apply them in different ways, like strikers, fullbacks and wingers. It is only by playing together as a team that they can be realised to best effect. N&P's insistence on team-play language was used to create a mind set of the new culture that they wanted to develop. The role of coach has evolved from team captain on the field of play to coach during periods of time out. Players also coach each other as a result of their team learning and through N&P's understanding process.

Good communication is actively promoted through the N&P understanding process which focuses on just that: everyone's understanding. Team events are held to ensure that all players are on board with the direction of the business. They follow a simple, common format based around key questions of 'What has not gone well that we can improve?', 'What has gone well from which we can learn?' and 'What ideas, issues or concerns have we got?' This emphasis on two-way communication enables N&P to react quickly to changes in the marketplace. Two weeks after a new mortgage offer was launched they were able to improve it as a result of direct and fast feedback through the understanding process – a remarkable achievement which prevented them scoring an own goal!

Their Quality of Management and Team Leadership programmes use internal facilitators to promote the society's management philosophy of making the most of the potential of people. Over 130 team leaders and players have become facilitators of these programmes. Players are rewarded for their contribution to team achievements not only in terms of renumeration but also in opportunities to develop greater competencies. Coaching has helped players to adjust to the organisational and cultural changes so that N&P has become a true learning organisation. As one of the Understanding Process Team says, 'In my 27 years with the society I have never seen it in better shape. We need everyone on board to achieve success and sustain our performance. Developing greater coaching capability in team-play has been one of the key factors in getting everyone moving in the same direction.'

East Midlands Electricity

East Midlands Electricity (EME) is one of the public utilities that were privatised in the early 1990s. The company's core electricity business has undergone a series of substantial changes since then. One of the main areas that EME has focused on is the need continually to improve customer service. Coaching staff through the changes has seen a greater acceptance of individual responsibility and sense of personal influence on the success of the business.

Geoff Wass, General Manager of the Leicestershire Business Unit, was one of the senior managers who undertook an individual achievement coaching programme. His commitment to developing a coaching approach has influenced the transition in management style from control towards coaching. Wass says, 'We have taken the safety harness away but not the safety net. The emphasis is on supporting individuals to make decisions whilst understanding the implications of their actions on the business and our customers.'

EME has moved to a flatter structure and reorganised the electricity business into seven business units. They are committed to creating an empowering environment and promoting teamworking. Coaching has supported the transition from being told what

147

to do to ensuring greater ownership and responsibility to make decisions. Their telephone answering bureau has now set itself the target of satisfying customer enquiries first time for 90 per cent of incoming calls. Instead of customers having to wait on hold for long periods or being passed around the organisation, the aim is for callers to be dealt with by the initial recipient of the call. Coaching has helped identify additional training requirements and areas to improve the service. Keeping the focus on the objectives for coaching has also helped the transition in management style. Promoting the sound business reasons for improving customer service and reducing costs are seen as essential in developing coaching capability. Allowing team members to develop and gain some initial experience before embarking on additional training in coaching skills and leading teams is seen as an important part of the process of development. Participants were also able to have input into the training design and identify benefits based on the context of their experience in the new structure.

EME has found that this approach has seen many individuals suddenly start to blossom in the new culture as they are freed to take initiatives. Promoting this empowering approach requires an acceptance of the risks involved. Says Geoff Wass, 'There is a lot of ongoing debate as the message is moved through the organisation. We have a greater understanding and acceptance that mistakes will be made, except in safety-critical areas where there is no room for mistakes.' The business management teams have found that this ongoing dialogue creates an atmosphere of trust in which empowerment can take place. This does not mean letting go of everything at once but a gradual move related to competence. Getting individuals to feel more comfortable and competent has raised their confidence to make decisions. Coaching has been a catalyst in making this happen.

References and Further Reading

BALLARD H. J. *Developing a Coaching Framework: An exploratory study*. University of Sheffield, 1991

BBC TRAINING VIDEOS. *Coaching for Results*, 1994

THE ENGINEERING COUNCIL. *Continuing Professional Development: The practical guide to good practice*. London, the Engineering Council, 1991

EVERED R. D. and SELMAN J. C. *Coaching and the Art of Management: Organisational dynamics*. New York, AMA Publications, 1989

HAMBLIN A. C. *Evaluation and Control of Training*. Maidenhead McGraw-Hill, 1974

HAMMER M. and CHAMPY J. *Re-engineering the Corporation*. London, Nicholas Brealey, 1993

HANDY C. *The Age of Unreason*. London, Business Books, 1989

— *The Empty Raincoat*. London, Hutchinson, 1994

— *Understanding Organizations*. Harmondsworth, Penguin, 1985

HARRI-AUGSTEIN S. and THOMAS L. F. *Learning Conversations*. London, Routledge, 1991

HUTHWAITE RESEARCHED EFFECTIVENESS. *20:20 Vision Survey Report*. Rotherham, Huthwaite, 1994

HUTHWAITE RESEARCH GROUP. *Coaching Skills and their Use as a Managerial Tool*. Rotherham, Huthwaite, 1990

INGLETON C. *Management Interviewing*. Special Interest Publications, 1988

JEROME P. J. *Coaching through Effective Feedback*. Richard Chang Associates, 1994

LABORDE G. Z. *Influencing with Integrity* Palo Alto, CA, Syntony Publishing, 1987

LYNCH D. and KORDIS P. L. *Strategy of the Dolphin*. London, Arrow Books, 1990

MORGAN G. *Creative Organisation Theory*. London, Sage Publications Ltd, 1989

NAISBITT J. and ABURDENE P. *Megatrends 2000*. London, Futura Publications, 1984

PEASE A. *Body Language*. London, Sheldon Press, 1981

PETERS T. and WATERMAN R. H. *In Search of Excellence*. New York, Harper Row, 1982

ROBBINS A. *Unlimited Power*. New York, Simon and Schuster, 1988

SALISBURY F. S. *Developing Managers as Coaches*. London, McGraw-Hill, 1994

SENGE P. M. *The Fifth Discipline*. London, Century Business, 1992

WHITMORE J. *Coaching for Performance*. London, Nicholas Brealey, 1992

Index